Lowcountry Delights

Cookbook & Travel Guide

First Printing
2002

A collection of recipes from
favorite Bed and Breakfast Inns, Historic Inns, and Restaurants
in The Lowcountry

Beaufort, South Carolina
Charleston, South Carolina
Savannah, Georgia

Maxine Pinson & Malyssa Pinson

SSD, Inc.
d/b/a
The INNside Scoop
innsidescoop.com
Savannah Restaurants Online
eatinginsavannah.com
The Food Scoop
thefoodscoop.com

Savannah, Georgia

Published by

SSD, Inc.

22 W. Bryan St.~~ PMB 202
Savannah, GA 31401

First Printing   May 2002   4,000 copies

Cover and Layout Design: Maxine Pinson
Copy Editor: Malyssa Pinson
Author Photo: Jason Chervenak
        GalleryByte.com
        Savannah, GA
Publishing Consultants: Patty Croft and Sheila Thomas
        The Wimmer Companies
        Memphis, TN

Library of Congress Control Number: 2002091142

Order forms for this book are on page 177.
They may be printed out from: www.thefoodscoop.com/LowcountryDelights.html

Disclaimer and Limits of Liability

While the authors and publisher have used their best efforts to insure the accuracy of all information at press time, changes do transpire. Therefore, SSD, Inc. does not guarantee the accuracy or completeness of any information and is not responsible for any errors or omissions or the results obtained from use of such information. The recipes included in this cookbook are favorites of the inns and restaurants; some are original (especially from the restaurants), but all are not. One or both authors has personally experienced each bed and breakfast or historic inn and restaurant included and highly recommends each. No payment was received for inclusion in the book. Most recipes were tested by the authors who edited each recipe for clarity. This book is sold as is without any warranty of any kind, either expressed or implied. Neither the authors nor SSD, Inc. or its distributors shall be liable to the purchaser or any other person or entity with respect to any liability, loss, or damage caused or alleged to be caused directly or indirectly by this book.

ISBN 0-9716662-0-2

WIMMER
COOKBOOKS

ConsolidatedGraphics
1-800-548-2537

❧❧❧❧❧❧❧❧❧❧❧❧❧❧❧❧❧❧❧❧❧❧❧❧❧❧❧❧❧❧❧❧❧

To Celia,
our much missed daughter and sister

To Billy,
our much loved husband and father

And to Lois,
our special friend

❧❧❧❧❧❧❧❧❧❧❧❧❧❧❧❧❧❧❧❧❧❧❧❧❧❧❧❧❧❧❧❧❧

The Scoop on Cowcountry Delights

The selection of the B & B's and Historic Inns, included in *Lowcountry Delights,* **was based upon the following criteria:**

- Hospitality and personal warmth of innkeepers
- Willingness to accommodate the requests of guests, when possible
- Professionalism of innkeepers
- Appearance of interior and exterior of inn
- Furnishings, style/design, room decor
- Attention to detail
- Distinctive features
- The quality and presentation of breakfast
- Amenities and conveniences
- Availability and upkeep of grounds or garden area
- Location of inn and consideration of area attractions
- Private baths
- Respect for the privacy of guests
- Telephones in room, preferred but not mandatory
- Value of accommodations and services received
- Historical significance, when applicable
- Honesty and congruency in marketing
  (Web site and brochure *accurately* represent the inn)
- The integration of each of the 5 senses (sight, sound, taste, touch, smell) into a unique inn experience

---

Note: *No payment was received for an inclusion in this book. We are discerning in the places we select, but we also make a concentrated effort to consider the tastes and preferences of others. Some of the inns and restaurants are big-time operations, others are family-run and operate on a smaller scale.*

The selection of the restaurants, included in *Lowcountry Delights*, was based upon the following criteria:

- Selection and uniqueness of menu
- Service and food knowledge by server
- Timely delivery of meal
- Presentation of meal
- Decor and ambience
- Friendliness of staff
- Location
- Value of meal for price paid

The Selection and Testing of Recipes included in *Lowcountry Delights*

The selection of recipes was, primarily, left up to the contributor. We requested recipes that were favorite dishes with their guests and clientele--preferably, ones not to difficult to prepare in a home kitchen. We did provide guidance, in the category of recipes, in order to prevent duplication and provide more variety. Even though some of the recipes are considerably more challenging to prepare than others, the ones we have persevered in preparing have been worth the effort.

The majority of the recipes have been tested, in a non-commercial kitchen, by us. We have added notes to some recipes which we have prepared, but not all. We have spent much time editing the recipes so that they are easy-to-follow and understand. Substitutions are included for hard-to-find ingredients or else guidance is provided for locating the item.

Why *Lowcountry Delights* is one-of-a-kind cookbook/travel guide

Our research reveals *Lowcountry Delights* is the only cookbook/travel guide, on the market, including all of the following features:

- Favorite local dining establishments recommended in locations of B&B's/ Historic Inns

- Basic information provided, at a quick glance, on each inn and restaurant

- A sketch or photograph of each inn or restaurant featured is included, enabling one to get a feel for its ambience in advance

- A section on dining etiquette

- A comprehensive Q & A section, for inngoers, laced with inntertaining inn-related anecdotes

Acknowledgements

With forever gratitude to...

Advisory Board Members, Tricia Ainsworth, Frances Davis, Mariette and Claude Gagne, Pamela Lanier, Emily Sarah Lineback, Jackie Morrison, Recipe Contributors, Jim and Carol Ruddick, Sandy Soule, Sheila Thomas, Marcia Thompson, Chip Ulbrich, and special friends who believed "we could and we would"--and who provided supportive encouragement from beginning to end. We extend heartfelt thanks to each of you.

A special salute goes to Patty Croft, with Wimmer cookbooks, without whose patient tutorial guidance *Lowcountry Delights* would still be an unformatted computer document. Patty, you may not be a "lowcountry delight," but you are a much appreciated delight.

Credits

Lee Morrison
Photograph of Charleston's bandstand on back cover

Theron Wallis
Illustrator of original artwork
(Beaufort, Charleston, Savannah, Oscar's, Bodi's,
Georges of Tybee, Soho South Cafe, Beach Dreams)

Middleton Place
for permission to use photograph of Middleton Oak

Beaufort Chamber of Commerce
for permission to use photograph of Beaufort on back cover

Charleston Area Convention and Visitors Bureau
for quotes on Charleston

Savannah Area Convention and Visitors Bureau
for quotes on Savannah

SavannahMenu.com
for permission to use photographs
(Johnny Harris Restaurant and Yanni's Greek Cuisine)

The Cover Photograph
(in addition to The Tidal Creek--p. 21, The Lowcountry Oaks--p. 160,
and The Napping Cat--p. 126) taken by Maxine Pinson at Laurel Hill Plantation

Advisory Board
for Innformation Section

෴෴෴෴෴෴෴෴෴෴෴෴෴෴෴෴෴෴෴෴

David and Wendy Adams
Adams Edgeworth Inn--Monteagle, TN
www.assemblyinn.com

Donna and Bob Marriott
Casa Sedona--Sedona, AZ
www.casasedona.com

Gale and Jim Chapman
Prestwould Bed & Breakfast--Flat Top, WV
www.prestwould.com

Celeste and Harry Neely
The Nicholson House--Athens, GA
www.nicholsonhouseinn.com

Collin Clarke
Mr. Mole Bed & Breakfast--Baltimore, MD
www.mrmolebb.com

Peggy Patteson and Bill Westbrook
The Hope and Glory Inn--Irvington, VA
www.hopeandglory.com

Harriet and Jim Gott
Bufflehead Cove Inn--Kennebunkport, ME
www.buffleheadcove.com

Gloria and Bob Rogers
Four Rooster Inn--Tabor City, NC
www.4roosterinn.com

Ruth and Jim Edwards
John Penrose Virden House--Lewes, DE
www.virdenhouse.com

Bonnie and Tom Sawyer
William Kehoe House--Savannah, GA
www.williamkehoehouse.com

Joe Finnegan
St. Francis Inn--St. Augustine, FL
www.stfrancisinn.com

Anne and Bob Washburn
The Chalet Club--Lake Lure, NC
www.chaletclub.com

Peggy and Tom Flint
Folly Castle Inn--Petersburg, VA
www.follycastle.com

Mary and Roger Wolters
Red Horse Inn--Landrum, SC
www.theredhorseinn.com

Ann and Keith Gay
Beach Dreams--Tybee Island, GA
www.beachdreamsbandb.com

Vikki Woods
Iron Mountain Inn--Butler, TN
www.ironmountaininn.com

Jackie and Lee Morrison
"Innkeepers Emeritus"
Laurel Hill Plantation Bed & Breakfast
(1986-2001)
McClellanville, SC

Note: *The Advisory Board consists of innkeepers whose inns have been reviewed or recommended by The INNside Scoop bed & breakfast newsletter. These inns par excellence, located in different areas of the country, are recommended with pride and pleasure. Photographs, of each inn, may be seen on pages 158-159. Deep appreciation is expressed, to each of these innkeepers, for their input and feedback on the Q&A section found on pages 134-156.*

About Cover Photograph

❧❧❧❧❧❧❧❧❧❧❧❧❧❧❧❧❧❧❧❧❧❧❧❧❧❧❧❧❧❧

Laurel Hill Plantation Bed and Breakfast
(1986 - 2001)

*W*hen the original Laurel Hill Plantation house was constructed in 1850, Richard Tillia Morrison (the current owner's great, great grandfather) owned more than 20,000 acres in the area. Laurel Hill was a turpentine plantation that produced lumber and naval stores. The Morrison family sold Laurel Hill in the 1950's, and the new owners used the land for truck farming. Except for short periods, when migrant workers stayed in the house, it was vacant.

For over 20 years, Jackie Morrison longed to own the abandoned house and begged the owners to sell it. They finally agreed to sell the house, but not the land. A stipulation was made that the house had to be moved, in its entirety, and the site had to be left in pristine condition.

In January 1983, Jackie and Lee Morrison moved the Laurel Hill Plantation House from Highway 17 to its present location on another part of the original plantation tract. Restoration of the dilapidated house moved slowly, but the results were remarkable. In May of 1985, Laurel Hill was listed on the National Register of Historic Places. A year later, Laurel Hill was featured in *Country Living* magazine. In July 1986, the Morrisons opened their country home as a bed and breakfast inn--a true Lowcountry delight.

On September 21, 1989, Hurricane Hugo hit the South Carolina coast with a twenty foot tidal surge and 200 m.p.h. winds. The house at Laurel Hill was destroyed--nothing was left. The Morrisons refused to give up their dreams and set about designing a replacement house, based on the plan of the lost house.

On July 1, 1991, Laurel Hill Plantation Bed and Breakfast was re-opened in the new structure. The Morrisons operated Laurel Hill as a B & B for fourteen years. They retired from innkeeping in January 2002.

An antique and gift shop, Antiques at Laurel Hill, is now located in the house and at a booth in Hungryneck Antique Mall in Mt. Pleasant, SC. Shopping at the Laurel Hill location is available by appointment. Visit **www.laurelhillplantation.com** for information about the mall location, or call 843-887-3708 to make an appointment to visit the Laurel Hill location.

Jackie is a past president (1999-2001) of the South Carolina Bed and Breakfast Association, and she continues serving on its board of directors.

Jackie and Lee have granted a conservation easement on Laurel Hill Plantation to The Nature Conservancy.

See pages 122-123 for a collection of Jackie Morrison's
Laurel Hill Plantation's B & B recipes and an order form for Jackie's cookbook.

Introduction

by Pamela Lanier

ઈષ ઈષ ઈષ ઈષ ઈષ ઈષ ઈષ ઈષ ઈષ ઈષ ઈષ ઈષ ઈષ ઈષ ઈષ ઈષ ઈષ ઈષ

*W*hen Maxine asked me to write the introduction to her cookbook I was thrilled, not only because Maxine is a wonderful supporter of bed and breakfasts, but also because Southern cooking, and especially Lowcountry cooking, is one of my very favorite cuisines. It's only natural, I guess, since I grew up in Tennessee and have spent many happy summers visiting family members on Lowcountry beaches. The whole area from Beaufort, South Carolina, to "the marshes of Glynn" resonate strongly throughout my family due, in part, to my forbear, the poet Sidney Lanier, whose poems so beautifully capture the magic of the area.

Beauty and magic abound in the Lowcountry, and the inns Maxine has chosen are perfect reflections of the area. What is most delightful about this book is that you have the opportunity to bring some of the inns' atmosphere home. Preparing these wonderful dishes in your own kitchen can fill your heart and home with the same warmth and pleasure kindled at the inn's table.

The warmth and pleasure of bed and breakfasts and country inns have fascinated me ever since I returned from a post-college trip to Europe where I stayed in B & B's and small inns. I was so captivated that I wrote a guidebook entitled *The Complete Guide to Bed & Breakfasts, Inns & Guesthouses.* I've just completed its 19th edition. What is it about these lodgings that I find so compelling? Why am I still enthralled after so many years in the industry?

Well, first of all, like a snowflake each inn is unique, shaped by the building's architecture and décor, the innkeepers' personalities, and the region in which it is located. With no two being alike, I am assured of a distinctly different, and inspiring, experience at each inn I visit. Secondly, I love to be pampered and to me breakfast in bed or tea served in my room is the ultimate in pampering. Just to lean back into the pillows sipping my tea and nibbling on a freshly baked muffin, perusing a magazine or gazing out a window at the surrounding coun-tryside--to me this is heaven.

And I do not think I am very different from most inngoers. After a hectic week at the office, they arrive at an inn ready for that pampering, enveloping environment and the unique experience that lets them know they are somewhere special, a place where they can shed the week and rejuvenate. Nothing says change of pace more for the average working person than to wake up ensconced in a feather bed surrounded by a beautiful, romantic ambience with the smell of coffee wafting upstairs. Here they can savor breakfast, the one meal of the day most busy folks do not have the luxury of enjoying. An assembly-line bagel scoffed down on the way to an early-morning meeting can hardly compare to the lavish, relaxing repast spread before them at a country inn.

Which brings me to the third reason I am still passionately involved in this industry--country inn cuisine. Being a great breakfast fan, the thrill of a new breakfast every morning in itself is enough to keep me going! And as the cuisine an inn serves is as unique as the inn itself, each meal is a new and exciting celebration of local ingredients and ambience. A successful inn cannot be separated from the region in which it is located, and the most successful inn cuisine reflects this regional character.

Sharing--recipes, stories, family photographs--is what brings guests and innkeepers together. Who can forget conversations around a gorgeous breakfast table amidst heaping platters of fresh fruit, home-baked breads, and fragrant egg dishes? What makes these meals so memorable is sharing joy and laughter with other guests and the innkeepers themselves. At that table, in that special inn, no one is a stranger, ages and occupations are not significant, barriers melt away as easily as warm butter on a stack of flapjacks.

Have I become jaded by bed and breakfasts? Never!

I hope you enjoy the beautiful and delicious recipes from Lowcountry inns--and imagine yourself nestled by the warmth of their hearths.

Bon Appétit!

Pamela Lanier
www.TravelGuides.com

Pamela Lanier is the author of The Complete Guide to Bed & Breakfasts, Inns and Guesthouses *(currently in its 19th annual edition), host of the Yahoo! Gold Star recipient web site TravelGuides.com, and editor of four bed and breakfast cookbooks.*

She also serves as director of Bed & Breakfast Inns and Guesthouses International, *with a membership of over 7,000 inns.*

Photo courtesy of Middleton Place--Charleston, SC

The Middleton Oak, located upon the magnificent grounds of Middleton Place outside Charleston, served as an Indian Trail tree long before Columbus discovered America. Overlooking the Ashley River, the Middleton Oak's enduring grace and beauty captures the essence of The Lowcountry and the captivating mystique that is uniquely hers.

Foreword

by Maxine Pinson

Maxine and Barrister II, the Pinsons' retired greyhound who found life and happiness by following the beat of a different drummer and running the "wrong" way

*L*iving in The Lowcountry, for the past thirty years, has been a highlight of my life. No matter where I go—in this country or abroad—when I say I am from Savannah, there is almost always instant recognition. Positive comments follow, and I feel proud and privileged to live where I do. The Lowcountry—boasting Beaufort, Charleston, and Savannah—is an uncommon place. The uniqueness of The Lowcountry is no longer a secret.

After publishing a parenting publication, for five rewarding years (1990-1994), I expanded to Beaufort and Charleston, SC. The publication became *Lowcountry Parent*, and I became enchanted with Beaufort and Charleston as well. It was during this time that I first began writing travel articles (using the name of an admired great-grandmother as a pseudonym) and recommending area restaurants to my readers.

Due to a series of crisis-level personal circumstances, I had to make the painful choice of discontinuing my parenting publication in the fall of 1995. At that point-in-time, I could no longer meet the demands of publishing *Lowcountry Parent* without compromising the high quality and service to which I was committed. To give less than my best was not something I was willing to consider. However, by then, publishing was in my blood. I knew I would never be able to give it up completely.

Since 1989, I have wanted to write a book, and I knew I would not rest in peace until that goal was accomplished. The last issue of my parenting publication came out in October 1995, and the first issue of *The INNside Scoop*—a bed and breakfast newsletter "Dedicated to the Discovery of Bed and Breakfast Getaways"—made its debut in December 1995. I had no concept, at that time, of the joys awaiting me as I moved forward into the next chapter of my life.

For the first five years, *The INNside Scoop* was a 4-page quarterly newsletter featuring bed and breakfast inns in Georgia and the Carolinas. Beginning in 2001, it became an 8-page bi-annual newsletter featuring inns in Georgia, the Carolinas, plus four additional states. I first became hooked on bed and breakfasts (see page 130) during 1971 when my husband, Bill, and I spent the summer in England. Since that time, I have had the opportunity of experiencing dozens of inns—large, small, and in-between—in all parts of this country and abroad. Each edition of *The INNside Scoop* now includes recommended bed and breakfasts and historic inns, in addition to recipes from inns I have previously visited. An inn in each state in the eastern United States has been reviewed by me, and I am now heading west.

How It Happened: "The Tracks of Max"

In the spring of 1989, at the lowest and loneliest point in my life, I heard a message that touched and changed my life forever. However, it was not until much later that I realized what a tremendous impact the content of the message had upon me. It sparked a growing desire within me to spend the rest of my life providing encouragement and hope to others.

I have always felt that good can evolve from evil, and this belief has brought me to where I am today. If it had not been for a personal trauma I experienced in 1989 (to be addressed, in detail, in future books), I never would have returned to my alma mater to take courses in journalism, speech, and technical writing. Little did I know what these courses were preparing me for. I only knew that taking them was something I felt inexplicably compelled to do, and I have always trusted my instincts. Seldom do they mislead me.

A few months after completing my courses, I was contacted by a publisher in Atlanta insisting that I accept the position of editor for a new parenting publication, *Savannah Parent*. I refused—twice. A few weeks after my second refusal, 20,000 copies of the new publication arrived in Savannah. I was listed as editor, although I had absolutely nothing to do with that edition. After 3 months, I had received no compensation, as promised, for my 60-plus-hour weeks. Well, actually, I did receive two checks. Each bounced. At that point, I'd had my fill, and that is when I took action. Long story made short: after sending a couple of letters and making a few phone calls, I did some bouncing—right into the position of owner, publisher/editor/ad representative/marketing director for *Savannah Parent* newsmagazine.

People often ask how I got started with *The INNside Scoop*. Now you have it—the inside scoop on *The INNside Scoop! Savannah Parent* is the grandparent of *The INNside Scoop*, which is the parent of *Lowcountry Delights* cookbook and travel guide. It is my hope that a writing ministry, launched with *52 Scrolls* (see page 167), will be the next offspring of this sequel.

In 1998, at the end of what I refer to as my "decade of hell," I lost my first child to a rare and vicious form of cancer. I am grateful for the time God entrusted her to us. She was only 23-years-old when she died. So young...

When Celia died, I felt a big part of me died with her. I survived, emotionally, by staying busy. I still do. Five months after losing Celia, remembering the message of hope, I applied and was accepted (as an extended campus student) at Union Theological Seminary-Presbyterian College of Christian Education in Richmond, Virginia. Union-PSCE is a theological institution of the Presbyterian Church (USA). No, I am not preparing to become a pastor. I am going to seminary (only a few courses left) preparing for a writing ministry through which I would like to recycle the hope, encouragement, and inspiration I have received from others.

But, hey! If we should ever meet, and I hope we will, don't you worry about having to deal with some proof-texting religious fanatic. I am very outspoken about the pushing or forcing of one's religion or personal ideology upon another person. Try doing it with me, and you'll never suspect I'm a seminarian! It is because of my intolerance of religiosity (based upon my "experience of '89"--see www.the-innside-scoop.com/spirabuse.htm) that I became interested in attending seminary. I wanted to learn more about my faith, but I did *not* want it shoved down my throat through shaming, blaming, or an indoctrination process.

Today some of my dearest and most cherished friends are innkeepers. I consider them a special "breed." As much as I love staying in their incomparable bed and breakfasts and historic inns, what I cherish most are the relationships which have formed as a result of a snoop named Max trying to get the facts--the *innside scoop* on their bed and breakfast or historic inns. I hope you know, my friends, how much I care about and appreciate you.

Jackie and Lee Morrison, whom I have taken the liberty of proclaiming as "innkeepers emeritus," know about hope and the encouragement it provides. The story of how they attained their inn (cover photo), only to have it decimated by Hurricane Hugo, can be read about on page 8. On the first page of a cookbook Jackie compiled, she pens: *Laurel Hill Plantation: 1850. Carried to sea by Hurricane Hugo—September 21, 1989; Rebuilt 1990-91.*

The Morrison's were devastated by their loss, as anyone would be. But Jackie and Lee did not permit their unfortunate circumstances to wash away their lives or zest for living. Instead, they rebuilt and started anew. The house they rebuilt is even better and stronger than the original structure. Perhaps our common "steel magnolia" resolve is why Jackie and I became close friends in such a short period of time. Neither of us is afraid of "telling it like it is."

Life has taken me on many journeys during these past years, and not all have led to pampering bed and breakfast inns. During this time I have enjoyed (and often over-indulged) in fine dining at its best. I have also gleaned "food for thought"--lessons in life allowing me to see human beings and material stuff through clearer lenses. It has been an invaluable experience of growth, including *unappreciated* growth around my waistline and derrière! And, yes, dealing with that is next on my never-ending agenda.

Even though I have sought wisdom and guidance from numerous individuals during this project, whatever success may ensue I credit, in full, to my "Editor-in-Chief"—the only one to whom I ultimately feel accountable for choices I make and actions I take. Jesus Christ. Striving to follow his example, in my private life as well as in the public arena, is the primary mission of my life.

It is my hope that *Lowcountry Delights* will guide you to delightful and memory-making journeys, introduce you to delectable new dishes, and maybe even leave you with a little "food for thought" en route to whatever your final destination in life may be.

May each of your sojourns leave you with a reservoir of delightful and lasting memories, and may all the calories consumed evaporate as you travel to your next adventure!

Maxine Pinson, Publisher/Editor
The INNside Scoop

Table of Contents

❦❦❦❦❦❦❦❦❦❦❦❦❦❦❦❦❦❦❦❦❦

Beaufort, SC

B&B's and Historic Inns

Restaurants

Charleston, SC

B&B's and Historic Inns

Restaurants

Charleston Area

B&B's and Historic Inns

Restaurants

Savannah, GA

B&B's and Historic Inns

Restaurants

Tybee Island, GA

B&B

Restaurant

Other Recipes

NOTE: For recipes listed in specific food categories, see index.

INNformation for INNgoers

Our Story

Other

Recipes

from

The Lowcountry's
Most Delightful Inns & Restaurants

*Good food and gracious hospitality
flow through The Lowcountry like a tidal creek*

Beaufort lands a coveted spot on the *2001 National Trust for Historic Preservation* list of "12 Distinctive Destinations" -- travel treasures providing "striking alternatives to Anyplace, USA."

USA Today names Beaufort, SC as "one of 10 great places to honeymoon -- or renew nuptial bliss -- for romantics seeking an All-American destination." The article refers to Beaufort as a "sleeper hit, a sweet coastal gem filled with sweet B & B's and the sweeping verandas of antebellum mansions."

-- *USA Today* (October 22, 2001)

Beaufort is one of 50 towns chosen for inclusion in the 2001 edition of *The 50 Best Small Southern Towns*. The guidebook selects small southern towns portraying a "gentler way of life." According to the authors: "Beaufort exudes charm. The many historic homes, built in the late 1800's and early 1900's, gracefully enhance the town's colorful character. Live oak trees, draped with Spanish moss, grace the brick walkways and narrow streets; the town commands spectacular water views in three directions. No wonder several movies have been filmed in Beaufort."

-- Gerald Sweitzer and Kathy Fields

Web Site for Beaufort, SC
www.beaufortsc.org

Beaufort

"Beauty by the Bay"

Original artwork by Theron Wallis

Typical scene in the enchanting moss-draped, history-filled community of beautiful Beaufort, SC

The Beaufort Inn

*Located in the center of Beaufort's Historic Landmark District,
The Beaufort Inn offers an impeccable sense of style
where great expectations are quietly met.*

Address: 809 Port Republic Street
Beaufort, SC 29902
(Historic District)
Telephone: (843)521-9000
Fascimile: (843)521-9500

E-mail: bftinn@hargray.com
Web Site: www.beaufortinn.com
Category: An Historic Inn
Owner: Associated Luxury Inns of Beaufort
Rates: $135-$235 (year-round)

Molasses Pecan Butter

2 pounds unsalted butter, room temperature
1 cup toasted pecans, finely ground
¾ cup maple syrup
¼ cup molasses
1 tablespoon salt

Cream butter in mixer, add remaining ingredients. Blend well.
Roll into tubes of wax paper and freeze. Use as needed.

Yield: 2½ pounds

Editors' Note: *This delicious butter, wonderful on biscuits, molds beautifully!*

Citrus-Scented Banana French Toast

5-6 ripe bananas, sliced
16 crusty slices of French bread
10 eggs
4 cups milk
3 tablespoons sugar
Grated rind of 2 oranges
1 tablespoon cinnamon
½ teaspoon allspice
¼ teaspoon cardamom
1 tablespoon vanilla extract
Butter for frying

Place banana slices between bread slices to make 8 banana sandwiches. Mix eggs and next 7 ingredients in a wide, shallow dish; whisk until smooth. Dip sandwiches into batter until thoroughly soaked. Fry sandwiches in butter until golden. Transfer to a buttered cookie sheet to keep warm.

Yield: 8 servings

"One of the Top Ten Most Romantic Inns in The USA"
-- *The Road Best Traveled*, 1998

"From check-in to check-out,
the Beaufort Inn is a haven of wonderful experiences."
-- Karen Lingo, *Southern Living Magazine*

*The Beaufort Inn was originally built in 1897,
as a second home, by a prominent attorney from Hampton, SC.
The guest rooms are named after local plantations
and distinguished individuals of historical significance.*

Craven Street Inn

This lovely Victorian home, built as a private residence in 1870, creates a new standard for casual, affordable elegance.

Address: 1103 Craven Street
Beaufort, SC 29902
(Historic District)
Reservations: 1-888-522-0250
Telephone: (843)522-1668
E-mail: cravenstinn@hargray.com
Web Site: www.cravenstreetinn.com

Category: B & B
Innkeepers: Paige Solomon
Rachel Kingcade
Owner: Associated Luxury Inns
of Beaufort
Rates: $125-$225 (year-round)

Spinach and Leek Quiche

1½-2 tablespoons olive oil or butter
1 medium leek (white and green parts),
trimmed and chopped
½ small onion
4 eggs
1 cup heavy cream
½ teaspoon salt

¼ teaspoon freshly ground pepper
A generous pinch of nutmeg
Dash of red pepper flakes
1 (6-ounce) bag fresh spinach,
coarsely chopped
4 ounces sharp Cheddar cheese, grated
1 pre-baked pie crust

Preheat oven to 375 degrees. In sauté pan, sauté leek and onion in oil or butter. In a large bowl, whisk eggs with cream and next 4 ingredients. When the leek and onions are translucent (not brown), add spinach and cook until just wilted. Add leek and spinach to egg mixture. Place the grated Cheddar into pie shell and cover with egg and spinach mixture. Bake until quiche is puffed and golden (about 30 to 40 minutes). Good served with oven-roasted potatoes.

Yield: 1 quiche

Editors' Note: *Frozen onions and spinach may be substituted for fresh.*

ଊଊଊଊଊଊଊଊଊଊଊଊଊଊଊଊଊଊଊଊଊଊଊ

Pear Coffee Cake

Topping

¼ cup butter
¼ cup flour
½ cup brown sugar

2 teaspoons cinnamon
1 cup pecans or walnuts,
   finely chopped

Using a fork or pastry blender, cut together first three ingredients. Mix in cinnamon and nuts.

Cake

½ cup butter
¾ cup sugar
2 teaspoons vanilla
2 fresh eggs
2 cups all–purpose flour
1 teaspoon baking powder

1 teaspoons baking soda
½ teaspoon salt
1 cup sour cream
2½ cups pears
   (peeled, cored, diced)

Cream butter and sugar until light; add vanilla and eggs. In a separate bowl, mix together next 4 ingredients. Add flour mixture to butter mixture, alternately, with sour cream. Fold in pears.

Assemble the topping and cake batter. Spread batter into a greased and floured 13 x 9-inch pan. Cover with topping. Bake at 350 degrees 40 minutes.

Yield: 16 servings

"Though less imposing than some, Craven Street Inn is particularly charming, in part because it's furnished in an elegant, but unfussy, Sea Island style--and because the innkeepers are attentive, friendly, and fun talking with."
— *The Washington Post* (October 2000)

Built as a single family residence in 1870, the house served as the residence of the Lipton family for almost 75 years. Mr. Lipton was the cobbler at Parris Island who made all the boots for the Marine Corps recruits.

The Rhett House Inn

A place full of history, romance, and relaxation
providing the simple pleasures of an authentic plantation house.

Address: 1009 Craven Street
Beaufort, SC 29902
(Historic District)
Reservations: 1-888-480-9530
Telephone: (843)524-9030
E-mail: rhetthse@hargray.com

Web Site: www.rhetthouseinn.com
Category: An Historic Inn
Owners/Innkeepers:
Steve & Marianne Harrison
Rates: $195-$325 (seasonal)

Southern Grits

1 cup coarse, stone-ground grits
4 cups water
2-4 tablespoons chicken-base paste*
2-4 tablespoons butter

Combine all ingredients. Cook over low heat for about an hour, stirring occasionally. Cover and put into refrigerator overnight. The next morning, resume cooking; add milk or half-and-half, as needed. Cook over low heat for about an hour.

Yield: 6-8 servings

Editors' Note: *Chicken-base paste* is available in the gourmet section of most grocery stores.*

Cheese Hot Bites

1 cup flour
2 cups shredded Cheddar cheese
½ cup butter
¼ teaspoon salt
½ teaspoon cayenne pepper
1 cup pecans, chopped

Cream all ingredients, except pecans, together by hand. Add pecans and continue creaming until well mixed. Roll into logs. Wrap logs in wax paper and chill in refrigerator overnight. Thinly slice and bake on an ungreased baking sheet 10 to 15 minutes in a 325 degree oven; do not brown. Sprinkle salt on wafers while still warm. Logs may be frozen.

Yield: 4 logs.

Editors' Notes: *Before baking, sprinkle with sesame seeds and paprika. Store in an airtight container.*

"One of the best inns in The South."
-- *Southern Living*

Also featured in *Travel & Leisure, Martha Stewart Living,* and *In Style Magazine.*

The Rhett House Inn dates back to 1820 when Beaufort was a prominent coastal town noted for its rich culture and politics. Restored after the War Between the States, the inn emulates the beauty and romance of the Old South.

The Beaufort Inn

Offering three exceptional dining experiences

Address: 809 Port Republic Street
Beaufort, SC 29902
(Historic District)
Telephone: (843)521-9000

Web Site: www.beaufortinn.com/
dining.html
Cuisine: Contemporary Southern
Executive Chef: Chip Ulbrich
Price Range: $16~$29

Beaufort Inn She Crab Soup

½ pound unsalted butter
1 small yellow onion, diced
1 tablespoon fresh garlic, chopped
1 cup flour
2 bay leaves
1 teaspoon fresh thyme, chopped
½ teaspoon nutmeg
1 tablespoon Worcestershire sauce
1 cup dry sherry

½ gallon whole milk
2 cups heavy cream
1 cup crab stock, clam juice (easiest),
or 2 tablespoons commercial crab base
1 pound crab (blue, preferred) claw meat,
picked clean of shell
¼ cup crab roe, cleaned
Salt and fresh black pepper, to taste

Melt the butter in a heavy-bottomed stockpot; sauté the onion and garlic for 5 minutes until softened. Stir in flour and whisk until smooth, creating a roux which will thicken the soup. Cook for 5 minutes. Add remaining ingredients, except for crab and roe; whisk thoroughly to remove all lumps. Bring to a boil and stir until thickened. Season to taste, using lots of black pepper and salt. After puréing crab and roe in a food processor, gently stir it into the soup mixture. Adjust consistency, if needed, by adding more milk.

Yield: 8~10 servings

Shrimp and Grits

1 pound large shrimp, peeled and deveined
¼ olive oil
1 tablespoon garlic, chopped
½ cup smoked tasso ham*, diced fine
½ cup sun-dried tomatoes, soaked, drained, and minced
½ cup dry white wine
2 cups heavy cream
2 tablespoons butter
Salt and pepper, to taste
Grits, cooked according to directions
Parmesan cheese

In a very hot sauté pan, sear shrimp in olive oil; stir constantly. Add next 3 ingredients and continue stirring. Deglaze with wine and add cream. Cook an additional 2 to 3 minutes. Remove shrimp to a serving dish; cover to keep warm. Continue cooking sauce until thickened. Add butter and adjust seasoning. Pour sauce over shrimp and serve over cooked grits flavored with Parmesan cheese.

Yield: 2 servings

Editors' Note: *Tasso ham can usually be found at upscale grocery stores or delicatessens. However, Italian cappacola, prosciutto, or slices from a country ham may be substituted.*

"Top Inn Dining" -- *Country Inns Magazine*

"A *must* dining experience"-- *The Atlanta Constitution*

"Four Stars Outstanding" -- *Savannah News* restaurant review

Bistro 205

Fine Dining in a Relaxed Setting

Address: 205 West Street
Beaufort, SC 29902
(Historic District)
Telephone: (843) 524-4994

Cuisine: American Continental
Executive Chef/Proprietor: Gary Lang
Price Range: $17-$26

Ginger-Dusted Ahi Tuna with Asian Peanut Sauce

6 ounces yellowfin tuna, Sushi grade
1 tablespoon ground ginger
Salt to taste

Ground black pepper
Sesame seeds
2 tablespoons canola oil

Dust tuna filets with ginger; lightly cover with salt and pepper. Sprinkle each side with sesame seeds and set aside until ready to cook.

Sauce for Tuna

1 cup soy sauce
3 tablespoons mirin wine
1 cup orange juice

1 tablespoon minced ginger
1 tablespoon creamy peanut butter

Mix all sauce ingredients in a bowl and whisk well. Add mixture to a sauté pan and heat until liquid starts to thicken. Be careful not to reduce too much as sauce will become overpowering.

Heat oil in a pan over high heat; add tuna when pan is just about to smoke. Sear each side until crust is formed. Be careful to maintain a nice, rare center.

Yield: 1 serving

Filet Mignon
with Potatoes Napoleon and Apple Bacon Spinach

8 ounces beef tenderloin steak, trim fat
Salt and pepper, to taste
½ baking potato, cut into "waffle" chips
½ purple potato, cut into "waffle" chips
2 ounces Stilton cheese

¼ apple
1 tablespoon butter
1 slice bacon
Fresh spinach leaves, 6 ounces

Salt and pepper filet. Grill to desired doneness.

Cut potatoes into "waffle" chips with a mandoline* and place on a sheet pan. Weight potatoes down with another sheet pan on top. Bake in a 350 degree oven for 30 minutes or until just brown. Layer potatoes with alternating layers of Stilton cheese. Bake for an additional ten minutes.

Finely dice apple. Melt butter in a frying pan and sauté apple until softened. Meanwhile, cook bacon. Drain and dice. When apple is soft, add bacon to pan. After apple-bacon mixture is hot, add spinach leaves and cook until wilted. Season with salt and pepper.

Layer one-half of the potatoes, all of the spinach, the remaining potatoes. Top with grilled filet tenderloin.

Yield: 1 serving

Editors' Note: *A mandoline is a small kitchen aid with various adjustable blades for slicing firm fruits and vegetables into varied shapes.*

*A new restaurant in Beaufort
and already a favorite with the locals--or anyone else who experiences it.*

Plum's Waterfront Cafe

Casual Dining on the Waterfront

Address: 904½ Bay Street
Beaufort, SC 29902
(Historic District)
Telephone: (843)525-1946

Cuisine: Eclectic American
Executive Chef: Joshua J. McLean
Price Range: Lunch/$5-$10
Dinner/$13-$22

Plum's Turkey Apricot Nut Salad

2 cups chopped, smoked turkey breast
¼ cup golden raisins
¼ cup dried apricots, roughly chopped
¼ cup toasted almonds (chopped)
½ cup medium onions, diced
½ cup Hellmann's mayonnaise
Salt and pepper to taste
Lettuce

Combine all ingredients and serve over lettuce.

Yield: 4-6 servings

Editors' Note: *We also enjoyed a variation of this salad substituting scallions for regular onions and slivered almonds for chopped almonds. This is a refreshing luncheon dish and attractive served atop curly green lettuce and garnished with sliced apricots.*

Grilled Filet with Brandied Maytag Chèvre

1 medium onion, thinly sliced	Small can of artichoke hearts
8 fresh garlic cloves	Salt and pepper, to taste
Olive oil	2 (8-ounce) filet mignons

Oil a sauté pan and bring to medium-high heat. Add sliced onion and sauté, cooking and stirring until the onion begins turning a golden brown. Allow onion to attain a dark brown color to fully release their natural sugars into the pan. Continue cooking until caramelization is reached. Submerge garlic cloves in olive oil and cook in a 450 degree oven until tender. Squeeze excess water out of artichoke hearts by taking handfuls and squeezing each handful individually. Lay the hearts onto a sheet pan and season with salt and pepper. Bake at 250 degrees until artichokes become crispy and golden around the edges.

Brandy Blue Chèvre Sauce

1 cup heavy cream	¼ cup Maytag blue cheese
¼ cup brandy	¼ cup chèvre

Add all ingredients together in a sauce pot and bring to medium heat, stirring constantly. When sauce begins to thicken, it is ready. Adjust the taste with salt, if needed.

Season filets with salt and pepper. Grill on charcoal or wood. Top each filet with caramelized onions, artichoke hearts, and garlic. Top with the sauce.

Yield: 2 servings

Chosen as Beaufort's "Best All-Round Restaurant"
by *Lowcountry Weekly* (1999 & 2000)

"A crowded little place with a waterfront deck that seems to do almost everything well." --*Washington Post (10/22/00)*

"The bustling Plum's Cafe boasts 'creative casual cuisine and a prime waterfront location'." --*Atlanta Constitution Journal (5-9-01)*

For the ninth consecutive year, readers of *Condé Nast Traveler* name Charleston as "One of the Top 10 Travel Destinations in North America." (2001)

≈≈≈≈≈≈≈≈≈≈≈≈≈≈≈≈≈≈≈

The Charleston, SC area receives distinction
in the October 2001 issue of *National Geographic Traveler*,
as one of the "Top 50 Places of a Lifetime: America."

≈≈≈≈≈≈≈≈≈≈≈≈≈≈≈≈≈≈≈

Bride's Magazine honors the Charleston area as a "Top U.S. Destination"
in its 2001 Worldwide Honeymoon Guide

≈≈≈≈≈≈≈≈≈≈≈≈≈≈≈≈≈≈≈

"Charleston will turn the head of the most arrogant modernist. The brick-paved street lined with cast-iron lamps, the rows of pastel-colored houses-all conspire to make the city one huge antique: British colonial with a warm Southern breeze."
--Conde Nast Traveler

≈≈≈≈≈≈≈≈≈≈≈≈≈≈≈≈≈≈≈

Charleston claims the top spot for the eighth consecutive year
on Marjabelle Young Stewart's "Most Mannerly" list. (2000)

≈≈≈≈≈≈≈≈≈≈≈≈≈≈≈≈≈≈≈

"Suddenly, a warm fresh breeze turns up our collars and causes the swags of moss to sway gracefully, like billowing curtains. There is something in the air. It is not the familiar tang of the sea or the perfume of Confederate jasmine, nor is it the pealing of church bells or the delicate rustle of palmetto fronds. It is romance."

- -Stephanie Fletcher for *The Buffalo News*

≈≈≈≈≈≈≈≈≈≈≈≈≈≈≈≈≈≈≈

"Everything living has to change with the times, and I, for one, am as glad Charleston is a living city as I am that it remembers the past. As long as it can hold on to both, it will always be a place we want to go." --Mel White for *National Geographic Traveler*

Web Site for Charleston, SC
www.charlestoncvb.com

Charleston
"Champion of Character and Charm"

Original artwork by Theron Wallis

The Battery captures the charismatic charm of Charleston

Ashley Inn

A true taste of The South set in a charming architectural treasure

Address: 201 Ashley Avenue
Charleston SC 29403
(Historic District)
Reservations: 1-800-581-6658
Telephone: (843)723-1848
E-mail: ashleyinnbb@aol.com

Web Site: www.charleston-sc-inns.com/
ashley/index.htm
Category: An Historic Inn
Owner: Barry Caroll
Rates: $89-$250 (seasonal)

Tut's Toffee

35 saltine crackers
2 sticks butter
1 cup brown sugar
1 (12-ounce) package semi-sweet chocolate chips
1 cup chopped pecans

Preheat oven to 350 degrees. Line a (10 x 15-inch) jelly-roll pan with aluminum foil or parchment paper. Place saltines (7 down and 5 across) in pan. Combine next 4 ingredients in a microwave-safe bowl. Microwave on high 3 to 4 minutes; stir thoroughly and pour mixture over crackers. Bake at 350 degrees for 20 minutes. Remove from oven and cover with chocolate chips. Smooth with spatula and sprinkle with nuts. Chill and break into bite size bits.

Yield: 4 dozen pieces

Editors' Note: *Easy and delicious! Store in airtight container.*

Peaches 'n Cream Stuffed Waffles

4 fresh peaches, peeled and thinly sliced
(may substitute frozen)--save some for garnish

Waffle Batter

4 cups waffle mix
1½ cups milk
1½ cups water
3 eggs
2 teaspoons vanilla
2 teaspoons orange extract

Mix all together.

Filling

12 ounces cream cheese
1 teaspoon orange extract
½ cup confectioners' sugar
Sprigs of mint, optional

Whip together with electric mixer.

Prepare waffles and spread 1½ tablespoons filling on one-half of waffle. Top with peach slices and fold over. Top with praline sauce and garnish with a dollop of sour cream, more peach slices, and a sprig of mint.

Praline Sauce

2 cups brown sugar
1 stick butter
½ cup water (or maple syrup)

1 cup whole pecans
½ sour cream

Combine ingredients and melt in a saucepan. Add ½ cup water (or maple syrup) to thin and 1 cup whole pecans.

Yield: 8 servings

"Charleston's Gourmet Breakfast Place"

Recipient of prestigious "1997 Carolopolis Award"

Featured in the nationally televised
"Country Inn Cooking with Gail Greco" on PBS.

*Built in 1832 by Alexander Black,
an inventor of rice and cotton processing equipment*

Fantasia

A classic Charleston single-house in Charleston's historic district

Address: 11 George Street
Charleston SC 29401
(Historic District)
Reservations: 1-800-852-4466
Telephone: (843)853-0201

E-mail: reservations@fantasiabb.com
Web Site: www.fantasiabb.com
Category: B & B
Owners/Innkeepers: Marty & Cathy Riccio
Rates: $95-$205 (seasonal)

Fantasia's Spicy Pecans

2 egg whites, slightly beaten
2 teaspoons water
2 (16-ounce) bags shelled pecans
1½ teaspoons salt
½ cup sugar

1 tablespoon cinnamon
¼ teaspoon nutmeg
¼ teaspoon allspice
¼ teaspoon ginger

Preheat oven to 300 degrees. Combine egg whites and water. Add nuts and toss to coat. Combine next 6 ingredients. Add to nuts and toss until coated. Place in single layer on lightly greased baking sheet. Bake for 20 to 25 minutes.

Yield: 15-20 servings

Editors' Note: *Put in a holiday tin for a special gift during the holidays.*

Marty's Italian Tomato-Basil Frittata

1 small Vidalia onion, thinly sliced
1 fresh tomato (ripe and juicy), diced
8 large eggs
¼ cup half-and-half

¼ cup grated Romano cheese
4-6 leaves of fresh basil
Salt and pepper, to taste

Sauté sliced onion in skillet until soft and tender. Dice tomato and cook with onions for two minutes. Combine remaining ingredients; add tomatoes and onions to egg mixture. Return mixture to skillet and cook until eggs begin taking shape, be careful not to over-brown bottom. Remove skillet from top of stove and place under broiler to finish the frittata. The frittata is done when eggs are lightly colored and set.

Yield: 8-10 servings

Editors' Note: *Chopped peppers (green and/or red) add variety to this excellent frittata.*

Known as the Mary Scott House, this single-house dwelling stands on land Miss Scott inherited in 1791 from her grandfather, Daniel Legare, one of Charleston's earliest developers.

Governor's House

*One of the most elegant and historically significant homes in Charleston,
a city whose past is part of its soul*

Address: 117 Broad Street
Charleston, SC 29401
(Historic District)
Reservations: 1-800-720-9812
Telephone: (843)720-2070
E–mail: governorshouse@aol.com

Web Site: www.governorshouse.com
Category: An Historic Inn
Owners/Innkeepers: Karen Spell Shaw
Robert Hill Shaw, III
Rates: $165 ~ $330

Baked Grapefruit

1 red grapefruit (ripe, but firm)
Honey

Brown sugar
Sherry, optional

Preheat oven to 350 degrees. Cut grapefruit in half and section with a
grapefruit knife. Brush tops of grapefruit with honey and sprinkle with
brown sugar. If desired, brush with sherry and then sprinkle on brown
sugar. Bake for 15 to 20 minutes until warm.

Yield: 2 servings

Editors' Note: *A wonderful first-course breakfast dish during the fall
and winter months. Garnish with a maraschino cherry or an edible
flower.*

Haystacks

1 (6-ounce) bag of Nestle's white chocolate chips
½ cup of pretzel sticks, broken into small pieces
½ cup Spanish peanuts
Dried cranberries, about a handful

Melt white chocolate chips in a double-boiler. Stir in remaining ingredients and mix well. Drop small spoonfuls of the mixture onto wax paper. Cool.

Contributor's Note: *Cranberries are wonderful for fall treats , but they may be substitued with another fruit or omitted.*

Yield: Approximately 3 dozen pieces

Editors' Note: *White chocolate chips may be melted in a microwave.*

"Check into Charleston's Governor's House Inn
and you may never want to check out."
--Karen Lingo, *Southern Living* (September 1999)

Over 200 years ago, during Charleston's Golden Age, this magnificent home was the residence of Governor Edward Rutledge, the youngest signer of the Declaration of Independence. Here, he and his wife, Henrietta Middleton, received some of the country's most prominent leaders.

Hayne House

An oasis of character and charm near The Battery.

Address: 30 King Street
Charleston, SC 29401
(Historic District)
Telephone: (843) 577-2633
E-mail: haynehouse@yahoo.com

Web Site: www.haynehouse.com
Category: B & B
Owners/Innkeepers: Brian & Jane McGreevy
Rates: $135-$285 (seasonal)

Robie's Sausage and Egg Casserole

1 pound bulk sausage (mild or spicy)
3 tablespoons butter
½ cup chopped mushrooms
1 cup cream or half-and-half
15 eggs
½ cup New York sharp Cheddar cheese, grated

Brown sausage in skillet; crumble and drain. Spread sausage in bottom of a casserole dish. Sauté mushrooms in butter; drain and mix with cream in a separate dish. Soft scramble eggs and layer on top of sausage. Spread mushroom/cream mixture over eggs. Sprinkle grated cheese over top. Cook at 350 degrees for 20 minutes or until cheese is melted and casserole is bubbly.

Yield: 8 servings

Editors' Note: *An egg substitute product may be used instead of fresh eggs. Garnish with fresh basil.*

❦❦❦❦❦❦❦❦❦❦❦❦❦❦❦❦❦❦❦❦❦❦❦

Mrs. Lacey's Pound Cake

3 sticks Country Morning blend margarine
3 cups sugar
6 eggs
3 cups cake flour
1 (8-ounce) carton sour cream
1 teaspoon vanilla

Do *not* preheat oven. Thoroughly grease and flour Bundt pan. Cream butter and sugar together. Add eggs one at a time, beating well after each. Alternately, add flour and sour cream. Add vanilla. Place pan in oven. Turn oven on and bake at 325 degrees for 1½ hours.

Contributor's note: We serve this at breakfast, a custom we enjoyed in many of the small hôtels de charme we've experienced in Paris. It is delicious with fruit.

Yield: 1 pound cake

Editors' Note: *For variety, other flavorings (i.e., almond, lemon, orange, rum) may be substituted for the vanilla.*

Featured in *In Style* magazine

Selected as one of the top three inns in Charleston
and the only one with a top-rated breakfast.
-- *Travel Holiday* (February 2002)

"This converted Georgian-style single house--true native architecture--
on the residential (read: "Old Money") part of King Street
is pure Charleston." -- Sherri Eisenberg, *Travel Holiday* February 2002

One of 73 pre-Revolutionary buildings remaining in Charleston.

Lowndes Grove Plantation

*Overlooking The Ashley River, Lowndes Grove Plantation
proffers 18th century living at its finest*

Address: 266 St. Margaret Street
Charleston, SC 29403
Telephone: (843)723-8438
Fascimile: (843)723-0444
E–mail: info@lowndesgrove.com

Web Site: www.lowndesgrove.com
Category: B & B
Owners/Innkeepers: Lex & Tina Opoulos
Rates: $125-165 (year-round)

Muesli with Fruit

1 cup mixed seasonal fruit (assorted berries, bananas, apples,
    pineapples, orange sections, pears, nectarines, etc.)
1 cup vanilla low-fat yogurt
½ cup muesli
1 teaspoon honey
1 tablespoon slivered almonds or cashews, toasted

Wash and cut mixed fruit into bite-sized pieces. Place prepared fruit in a large
cereal bowl, add yogurt, and top with the muesli. Drizzle with honey; sprinkle with
almonds or cashews.

Yield: 1 servings

Editors' Note: *Muesli is a cereal found in most food and health food stores.
Raspberries and blueberries make a tasty and colorful fruit combination.*

Peanut Butter and Banana French Toast

¼ cup cool water
½ teaspoon vanilla extract
3 eggs, beaten
2 teaspoons peanut butter
4 slices egg bread (challah)

1 tablespoon margarine
2 bananas, peeled and sliced
    into ½-inch chunks (reserve
    some for garnish)
2 tablespoons real maple syrup

In a shallow bowl (like a soup bowl) beat water and vanilla into eggs until well-mixed. Spread a teaspoon of peanut butter onto two slices of bread and dip into egg mixture. Then take the other two slices and dip them into egg mixture. Heat margarine in a large frying pan over medium-high heat. When margarine starts bubbling, add the peanut butter slices into the skillet with the peanut butter side up.

Quickly lay out banana pieces onto the peanut butter and top with a slice of egg-dipped bread. Squish the sandwich together with a spatula. Let cook for about 3 minutes on first side and then cook for another few minutes on the other side. After 6 or 7 minutes of cooking, if sandwich seems too moist, cover pan with a lid and let cook an additional minute or two. Turn out the French toast sandwiches onto big plates, topped with a few thoughtfully placed banana slices. Serve with maple syrup.

Yield: 2 servings

Editors' note: *For a delicious, crunchy variation, roll sandwich in Corn Flakes before browning.*

"Offers closest thing you will find to experiencing what life
must have been like for the spoiled planter class
that ruled the antebellum South.
— Steve Bailey, *The Boston Globe* (1999)

Lowndes Grove Plantation was selected in 2001
as the setting for a photo-shoot by Tiffany and Company,
headquartered in New York City,
to convey the lifestyle of Tiffany's clientele.

The only surviving plantation on the historic Charleston penisula, Lowndes Grove Plantation is listed in the National Register of Historic Places and known as one of "Charleston's 62 most famous homes."

Two Meeting Street

Charleston's oldest and most renowned inn

Address: 2 Meeting Street
Charleston, SC 29401
(Historic District)
Telephone: (843)723-7322

Web Site: www.twomeetingstreet.com
Category: An Historic Inn
Owners/Innkeepers: Jean & Pete Spell
Rates: $165-$310

Baked Pears

9 pears
2 sticks butter
8 ounces jar mango chutney
1 cup raisins
1 teaspoon cinnamon

Cut pears in half and core. Mix remaining ingredients in a bowl. Stuff 1 teaspoon of butter mixture into each pear. Bake at 350 degrees for 20 minutes. Serve warm.

Yield: 9 pears

Editors' Note: *This mixture may also be used for stuffing apples (leave whole and core). Fruit used may be microwaved until tender and then baked in oven; baste with liquid. Serve stuffed fruit with dairy topping for a tasty dessert.*

Cucumber Spread

1 (8-ounce) package of cream cheese
1 stick butter
1 medium cucumber (peeled, seeded, and grated)
½ teaspoon garlic power

Combine all ingredients. Place in a small glass bowl and serve with crackers or assorted vegetables.

Yield: 1-1½ cups

"Best in the South"
-- *Southern Living* magazine poll
(1999 & 2000)

In the words of one writer,
"On a scale of one-to-ten for elegance,
Two Meeting Street is at least a twelve."

Featured in *Southern Accents, Southern Living, Travel and Leisure, Country Living, Harper's Hideaway Report, Country Inns and Gourmet,* and served as host for The Discovery Channel's "Great Country Inns of America" series.

The beautiful Queen Anne mansion, given as a wedding gift and completed in 1892, has welcomed guests from all over the world for over 65 years.

Wentworth Mansion

To step through its doors is to step into a world of refinement

Address: 149 Wentworth Street
Charleston, SC 29401
(Historic District)
Reservations: 1-888-466-1886
Telephone: (843)853-1886

Web Site: www.wentworthmansion.com
Category: An Historic Inn
Innkeeper: Bob Seidler
Rates: $315-$695

Cheese Sticks

5 cups all-purpose flour
3¾ teaspoons baking powder
3¾ teaspoons salt
2½ teaspoons cayenne
2½ teaspoons gumbo filé
1¼ teaspoons black pepper

2½ teaspoons granulated garlic
1½ cups unsalted butter,
   (cut into small pieces)
5 cups white Cheddar cheese,
   shredded
¾ cup grated Parmesan cheese

Mix first seven ingredients together. Whip the butter and cheese together; add the flour mixture, incorporating it until dough forms a ball. Wrap with plastic wrap and chill for 30 minutes or up to 2 days.

Preheat oven to 325 degrees. Roll out dough on a lightly floured surface to ⅛ inch thick. Cut dough into strips and transfer to an ungreased baking sheet, spacing strips 1½ inches apart. Bake for 12 to16 minutes or until golden brown. Allow sticks to cool; serve immediately.

Yield: 40 servings

Editors' Note: *Top with toasted sesame seeds and sprinkle with paprika. Dough may be frozen and used later.*

Bed & Breakfasts and Historic Inns
Charleston, South Carolina

Sticky Buns

1½ ounces yeast	1 ounce of non-fat milk solids
8 ounces water	3 eggs
4 ounces butter	1 pound bread flour
4 ounces sugar	4 ounces cake flour
Pinch of salt	

Preheat oven to 375 degrees. All ingredients should be room temperature. Place yeast in a small amount of the water using a separate container. In a mixer, combine next 4 ingredients until well-creamed. Add eggs, one at a time, until incorporated; add water and mix briefly. Add flour and then yeast mixture to the bowl; mix until smooth. Cover dough with plastic wrap and allow to rise for 1½ hours.

Scale dough into equal parts. On a floured work surface, roll each piece of dough into a 9 x 12-inch rectangle about ¼ inch thick. Brush off any excess flour. Next, brush surface of dough with softened butter and sprinkle with a mixture of cinnamon and sugar. Roll dough up so that it looks like a 12-inch long log. Cut log roll into 1-inch circular rolls and place on a pan with the honey pan glaze and pecan pieces smeared onto the bottom of it. Bake for 12 to 15 minutes or until golden brown. Allow buns to cool slightly and invert them onto a plate to be served.

Honey Pan Glaze

10 ounces brown sugar	2½ ounces corn syrup
4 ounces butter	1 ounce water
2½ ounces honey	

Cream together first four ingredients in a mixer. Add enough water to bring the mixture to a spreadable consistency.

Yield: 12 sticky buns

"Hideaway of the Year" -- *Andrew Harper's Hideaway Report* (December 1999)

One of the "50 Best Secrets" -- *Travel Holiday's* Insider Awards (September 1999)

"Inn of the Month" -- *Travel & Leisure* (November 1998)

Built in 1886 and designed in the Second Empire style as an opulent private residence by a wealthy cotton merchant, the Wentworth Mansion is now one of the world's finest and most unique inns--a pristine example of America's Gilded Age.

82 Queen

Eleven dining areas and a picturesque garden courtyard

Address: 82 Queen Street
Charleston, SC 29414
(Historic District)
Telephone: 1-800-849-0082
(843)723-7591

Web Site: www.82queen.com
Cuisine: Authentic Lowcountry cuisine
Proprietor: Chef Stephen G. Kish
Price Range: Lunch/$8-$13
Dinner/$16-$22
Cookbook: *The Best of Lowcountry Cuisine*

Grilled Portabella Mushrooms

Chèvre (goat's cheese)
4-6 portabella mushrooms (5" diameter with stems removed)

Gourmet greens

Marinade

2 cups oil
2 sprigs rosemary
1 teaspoon salt

1 teaspoon black pepper
1 teaspoon garlic

Vinaigrette

3 teaspoons balsamic vinegar
1 teaspoon olive oil
1 teaspoon brown sugar

1 dash salt
1 dash pepper

Mix all ingredients for marinade in shallow pie pan. Place mushrooms in pan and cover with marinade; marinate for 1 to 2 hours or overnight. Mushrooms will absorb most of the marinade. Grill mushroom 5 to 8 minutes per side, cook until tender. Remove, slice and plate top with vinaigrette. Garnish with goat's cheese and serve on a bed of gourmet greens.

Yield: 4-6 servings

Editors' Note: *A savory side dish for grilled steak or pork.*

McClellanville Crab Cakes

1 pound lump crabmeat, picked	1 dash of Worcestershire sauce
½ cup mayonnaise	½ cup coarse bread crumbs
2 green onions, chopped fine	½ ounce fresh lemon juice
2 dashes of Tabasco sauce	½ teaspoon ground thyme

Combine above ingredients thoroughly. Form into desired cake size (about 4 ounces).

Egg Wash

2 eggs   ¼ cup of half-and-half

Make egg wash with 2 eggs and half-and-half. Dip crab cakes into egg mixture, then roll into more bread crumbs. Sauté in butter or olive oil until golden brown. Serve with roasted red pepper cream sauce.

Yield: 4 crab cakes

Roasted Red Pepper Cream Sauce

4 ounces margarine	2 red bell peppers (seeded,
4 ounces flour	peeled, roasted, puréed)
2 cups milk	¼ teaspoon cayenne pepper
2 cups fish stock	Salt and white pepper to taste
¼ cup sherry	1 teaspoon paprika

In a saucepan, melt margarine over low heat. Add flour and whisk until it makes a pastry roux. Add next 3 ingredients and bring to a boil. Reduce heat and simmer. Add red peppers and remaining ingredients. Simmer 10 minutes; strain through a strainer. Add more milk, if too thick.

Yield: 6 servings

Editors' Note: *Crab cakes are a Lowcountry favorite, and these are superb.*

"Reigning in Charleston today--as it has for over fifteen years--is a place renowned in the culinary world for its simplicity and complexity; its grace and casual air; its hearty tables, napery, crystal and decor, coupled with a presentation of food, wine and service so divine as to be, itself, a work of Southern Fiction." --*Hospitality Today*, 1998

"Readers' Choice Awards – Best City Restaurant"
-- *Southern Living* (1997, 1998, 1999)

Blossoms Cafe

A high-energy, contemporary space that perfectly complements the cuisine

Address: 185 E. Bay Street
(Historic District)
Telephone: (843)722-9200
Web Site: www.magnolias-blossom.com/
Blossom/blossom.html

Cuisine: American Cuisine with
an Italian flair
Executive Chef: John Conneley
Price Range: Lunch/$9~$13
Dinner/$16~$27

Pan-Seared Mahi with Tomato-Basil Couscous

Couscous

2 cups strong vegetable stock
(chicken stock may be substituted)
½ cup couscous

2 tablespoons diced tomato
2 tablespoons fresh basil
Salt and pepper to taste

Bring the stock to a boil in a medium saucepan. Add remaining ingredients and stir; remove from heat and allow to sit for 3 to 5 minutes. Fluff with a fork. Set aside, but keep warm.

Caper Butter Sauce

1 tablespoon lemon juice
1 shallot, diced
1 tablespoon capers, chopped

¼ cup heavy cream
8 ounces butter, room temperature
Salt and pepper

Place first 3 ingredients in a small sauce pan over medium heat. Allow to reduce until liquid is almost gone. Add cream and reduce until thick. Reduce heat to low and slowly stir in butter, a little at time. Season with salt and pepper. The sauce may be made a few hours ahead, but keep it between 60-80 degrees.

Mahi Mahi

Olive oil (about 2 tablespoons)
½ cup all-purpose flour

Salt and pepper
2 (6-ounce portions) mahi mahi

Cover bottom of an ovenproof frying pan with olive oil. Season flour with salt and pepper. Lightly dust fish in seasoned flour and sauté in olive oil until golden brown. After turning the fish, place pan in a 350 degree oven for 5 minutes. Serve fish over couscous and cover with caper butter sauce.

Scallopini of Veal with Marsala Wine Sauce, Mushrooms, Prosciutto Ham, and Dried Tomatoes over Angel Hair Pasta

1½-2 pounds veal top round or pounded scallopini
   (3 pieces per person, 1¾ ounces per piece)
Salt and pepper, as needed

½ cup flour
Olive oil blend, as needed

Slice veal into 1¾ ounce pieces; cover with plastic and pound with a mallet to tenderize and flatten. Do not pulverize. Season veal with salt and pepper. Dredge in the flour, shaking off excess. Sauté in oil blend 3-4 pieces at a time, cooking (over even heat) just until done. Be careful not to burn caramelized bits that may accumulate on bottom of pan. Place veal on a plate until all is cooked.

Sauce

3 tablespoons olive oil blend
½ cup shallot, minced
2 teaspoons garlic, minced
½ cup shiitake mushroom caps, julienned
½ cup crimini mushrooms, quartered
4 ounces prosciutto ham, sliced

1 cup Marsala wine
2 cups browned, veal stock, reduced
¼ cup basil, fresh, julienned
⅓ cup dried tomatoes, julienned
Salt and black pepper, to taste

Add oil to pan used for cooking veal. Sauté shallots with garlic until translucent; add mushrooms and cook another minute. Add ham and deglaze with wine, reducing by two-thirds. Add remaining ingredients. Reduce by one-third over medium high heat. Add cooked veal to sauce, with all juices, until heated through.

Pasta

8 ounces angel hair pasta, fresh
3 tablespoons whole butter
1 teaspoon chopped garlic

3 tablespoons assorted chopped herbs (parsley, basil, chives, chervil, oregano)

Toss the just-cooked pasta with remaining ingredients. Place a nest of pasta at the top of the plate shingling 3 pieces of veal in front of it. Coat with sauce.

Yield: 4

Editors' Note: *If specified mushrooms are unavailable, substitute others that are.*

"When the revered Magnolias Uptown/Down South opened a spin-off Blossom Cafe, the question isn't whether to try it, but when!"
    --*Town & Country Magazine*

Joseph's

Family-operated and a favorite with the locals

Address: 129 Meeting Street
Charleston, SC 29401
(Historic District)
Telephone: (843)958-8500
Web Site: www.americascuisine.com/
charleston/josephsinfo.html

Cuisine: American eclectic
Executive Chef: Joseph Passarini
Price Range: Breakfast/$5.50~$8.95
Lunch/$5~$12
(Only breakfast served on Sundays)

Penne Pasta with Chicken

Oven-Dried Roma Tomatoes

12 Roma tomatoes, oven-dried
½ cup olive oil
½ cup balsamic vinegar

2 tablespoons fresh basil, chopped
4 tablespoons fresh garlic, chopped
(reserve 2 tablespoons)

Cut tomatoes in half and place on a cookie sheet with skin side down. Combine remaining ingredients and drizzle over tomatoes. Roast in a 500 degree oven for about 30 minutes. Turn oven off for 1 hour.

Chicken and Pasta

Olive oil
2 tablespoons garlic
4 boneless chicken breasts, grilled
12 oven-dried tomatoes

Pinch of fresh basil
1 pound fresh spinach
1 pound penne pasta, cooked
Splash of white wine

Heat olive oil in a large frying pan and sauté 2 tablespoons garlic, on high heat, with chicken, oven-dried tomatoes, and a pinch of basil until thoroughly heated. Add remaining ingredients. Cover and turn off the heat for about 2 minutes, or until spinach is wilted.

Yield: 4 servings

Fried Green Tomatoes with Sweet Citrus Rémoulade

Dust

2 cups all-purpose flour
1 teaspoon salt
1 teaspoon black pepper

½ teaspoon cayenne pepper
1 teaspoon garlic powder
1 teaspoon onion powder

Blend together and set aside.

Tomatoes

4 large green tomatoes,
   cut into thick slices
1 cup flour

3 whole eggs, beaten
4 cups dust
Vegetable oil, for frying

Dust tomatoes in plain flour, in eggs, then into dust. Fry at 350 degrees until golden brown. Drain on paper and serve hot with rémoulade.

Sweet Citrus Rémoulade

2 cups mayonnaise
1 teaspoon Worcestershire sauce
Pinch of salt and pepper
2 tablespoons lemon juice
1 teaspoon paprika

1 tablespoon green sweet relish
Handful of fresh parsley
1 tablespoon grained mustard
1 tablespoon capers

Put all ingredients into food processor and blend for about 30 seconds. Chill.

Yield: 4 servings

"Breakfast and lunch never tasted so good."
— *The Post and Courier*

"Unpretentious...superb."
— *The New York Times*

The Passarini family takes great pride in the quality, consistency, and honesty of their food and service.

Magnolia's

A unique blend of historic charm and contemporary excitement

Address: 185 E. Bay Street
Charleston, SC 29402
(Historic District)
Telephone: (843)577-7771
Web Site: www.magnolias-blossom.com/
magnolias2.html

Cuisine: New Southern cuisine
Executive Chef: Donald Drake
Price Range: Lunch/$7-$16
Dinner/$18-$28
Cookbook: *Magnolias Uptown/
Down South Southern Cuisine*

Creamy Tomato Bisque with Lump Crabmeat and a Chiffonade of Fresh Basil

¼ cup, plus 1 teaspoon, extra virgin olive oil
½ cup chopped yellow onion
1 teaspoon chopped garlic
½ cup flour
3 cups chicken broth, divided
1 chicken bouillon cube
4 cups homemade tomato sauce
 or 2 (4½-ounce) cans of tomato sauce
2 cups tomato juice

3 large peeled fresh vine ripened tomatoes
 or 1 (14½-ounce) can whole peeled
 tomatoes, crushed with juice
¾ cup thinly sliced fresh basil,
 loosely packed (save ¼ cup for garnish)
1 cup heavy cream
½ teaspoon salt
Dash of white pepper
8 ounces fresh lump crabmeat, picked clean

Heat olive oil over medium heat in a heavy bottomed stockpot. Add chopped onion and garlic. Sauté for 2-3 minutes, stirring until onions are translucent. Reduce heat and make a roux by adding flour and stirring until well-blended. Continue cooking over low heat for 5 minutes, stirring constantly. Turn heat up to medium and add 1½ cups of broth, stirring vigorously. Stir constantly until broth begins thickening and is smooth. Gradually add remaining 1½ cups broth and bouillon cube, stirring constantly until broth re-thickens. Reduce heat to low and simmer 5 minutes to cook out starchy flavor. Add next 4 ingredients and simmer 10 minutes. Skim off any foam collected on the top; add cream. Bring to a simmer and skim again, if necessary. Taste and add salt and pepper, if needed. When ready to serve, warm soup bowls. Garnish by sprinkling crabmeat and remaining ¼ cup basil over the soup. Serve immediately.

Yield: 8 (10-ounce) servings

Carpaccio of Fried Green Tomatoes
with Tomato Salad, Goat Cheese, and Tomato Chutney

Tomato Chutney
(combine all ingredients)

1 cup onions, julienned
2 cups cider vinegar
2 cups sugar

3 cups Roma tomatoes,
  julienned with seeds removed
2 tablespoons red pepper flakes

Tomatoes

1 egg, beaten
1 cup buttermilk
1 bottle Tabasco sauce
12 green tomatoes, thinly sliced

1 cup seasoned flour
2 cups Panko bread crumbs
3 cups fry oil

Beat egg, buttermilk, and Tabasco in bowl. Dip tomato slices in flour, shake off. Place tomato slices in buttermilk mixture and coat with bread crumbs. Fry in hot oil until brown.

Tomato Salad
(combine all ingredients)

1 cup cherry tomatoes
1 cup yellow tea drops
1 cup Dixie Dew drops
½ cup red onion, julienned
½ cup yellow pepper, julienned
½ cup fresh basil, chopped
  (save some for garnish)

1 tablespoon garlic
½ cup olive oil
½ cup red wine vinegar
Salt and pepper to taste
Goat cheese, crumbled

Place tomato chutney in center of plate. Top with 3 fried tomato slices and a generous serving of the tomato salad. Garnish with basil and cheese.

Yield: 4 servings

"Magnolia's, perhaps the city's most celebrated restaurant."
--- *Southern Living*

"Magnolia's a smart uptown space, specializes in updated Southern Food."
---*The New York Times*

"The hot spot in town . . .the restaurant is contemporary and upbeat."
-- *Detroit Free Press*

Middleton Place

Dining with spectacular views of the gardens at world-famous Middleton Place

Address: 4300 Ashley River Road
Charleston, SC 29414
Telephone: (843)556-6020
Web Site: www.middletonplace.org/
html/restaurant.html

Cuisine: Lowcountry plantation fare
Executive Chef: David Porter
Price Range: Lunch/$5.95-$12.95
Dinner/$15.95-$21.95

Warm Turkey Salad

1 turkey breast
Vinaigrette dressing
Mixed greens

Small bunch of grapes, red or green
½ cup pecans, chopped

Roast turkey breast and cool. Pull turkey apart. Marinate turkey in vinaigrette dressing and heat slowly. Serve over mixed greens topped with grapes and chopped pecans.

Vinaigrette Dressing

⅔ cup olive oil
⅓ cup apple cider vinegar
1 teaspoon salt
1 teaspoon sugar
½ teaspoon ground black pepper
½ teaspoon dry mustard
1 garlic clove, minced

1 teaspoon onion, minced
⅓ cup celery stalk, minced
½ green bell pepper, minced
½ red bell pepper minced
2 teaspoons parsley flakes
½ teaspoon thyme

Mix all ingredients together.

Yield: 6-8 servings

Corn Pudding

2 cups yellow corn
2 whole eggs
¾ quart of heavy cream

¼ teaspoon nutmeg
Pinch of salt and white pepper

Place yellow corn in a greased casserole pan. Mix all other ingredients together. Pour mixture over corn and bake for 45 minutes at 350 degrees or until golden brown.

Yield: 6-8 servings

Editors' Note: *Goes well with turkey and ham at Thanksgiving.*

Huguenot Torte

3 whole eggs
2 cups sugar
1 cup flour
½ teaspoon baking powder
½ teaspoon salt

4 Granny Smith apples, chopped
4 cups pecans chopped
½ teaspoon vanilla extract
Whipped cream, optional

Beat eggs until frothy and lemon colored. Add remaining ingredients and mix well. Pour into a greased sheet pan and bake at 325 degrees for 15 to 20 minutes.

Yield: 8-10 servings

Editors' Note: *Yummy served with whipped cream and festive garnished with a sprig of mint.*

Middleton Place, a National Historic Landmark and carefully preserved 18th-century plantation, has survived the American Revolution, the Civil War, earthquakes, and hurricanes. It has been home to many generations of the Middleton family beginning with Henry Middleton, President of the First Continental Congress; his son Arthur, a signer of the Declaration of Independence; his grandson Henry, Governor of South Carolina and an American Minister to Russia; and his great-grandson William, a signer of the Ordinance of Secession. Today the plantation (including extensive gardens, the plantation stables, and the house museum) is owned and operated by Middleton Place Foundation.

McCrady's

*McCrady's perfectly combines Charleston's love of history
with its hunger for new ideas*

Address: 2 Unity Alley
Charleston, SC 29401
(Historic District)
Telephone: (843)577-0025

Web Site: www.mccradysrestaurant.com
Cuisine: Contemporary American
Executive Chef: Michael Kramer
Price Range: $18-$29

Hearts of Palm Salad

Walnut Vinaigrette

¼ cup Dijon mustard
⅛ cup honey
¾ cup red wine vinegar
¼ cup lemon juice

½ cup walnut oil
1 cup canola oil
1 teaspoon finely chopped rosemary
Salt and pepper, to taste

In medium-sized mixing bowl, add first 4 ingredients. Slowly drizzle in oils until emulsified. Add remaining ingredients. Set aside.

Salad

½ pound mixed baby lettuces
Salt and pepper, to taste
¼ pound fresh hearts of palm, blanched

½ cup goat cheese crumbled
½ cup candied walnuts
¼ cup cucumber (seeded
and sliced into ¼ inch

Dress greens well; season with salt and pepper. Place greens on plate, top with hearts of palm, sprinkle with goat cheese, candied walnuts and cucumber.

Yield: 4 servings

Grilled Veal Tenderloin

Sauce

4 cups red wine
4 tablespoons sugar
2 tablespoons Madeira

Salt and pepper, to taste
2 tablespoons butter, softened

Place first 3 ingredients in a small saucepan over medium heat. Reduce to ⅛ cup. Add remaining ingredients. Set aside and keep warm.

Vegetables

2 tablespoons butter
2 large portabello mushrooms,
   cut into 1-inch pieces
1 bunch asparagus tips, blanched

8 red potatoes, roasted
2 sweet potatoes, peeled, cut into
   1-inch cubes and roasted
Salt and pepper, to taste

Melt butter in a large saucepan. Add mushrooms and cook until soft, about 3 minutes. Add remaining vegetables; season with salt and pepper. Set aside and keep warm.

Veal

4 (6-ounce) veal steaks   Salt and pepper, to taste

Heat grill to medium-high heat. Season all sides of veal well with salt and pepper. Place on grill at "10 o'clock" position; after 3 minutes, turn to "2 o'clock" to achieve a criss-cross pattern. Turn veal over and repeat. Set aside and keep warm. To serve, place vegetables on center of the plate with a cordon of sauce around the vegetables. Center veal on top.

Yield: 4 servings

Featured as one of *Esquire Magazine's* "Best New Restaurants of 1999."

Awarded the "Wine Spectator Award of Excellence"
(2000 & 2001)

Built in 1778, McCrady's is housed within one of the oldest existing taverns in the United States. During George Washington's southern tour in 1791, a party was held for him in The Longroom.

Poogan's Porch

Charleston's oldest award-winning restaurant

Address: 72 Queen Street
Charleston, SC 29402
(Historic District)
Telephone: (843)577-2337
Web Site: www.poogansporch.com

Cuisine: Lowcountry cuisine
Executive Chef: Nick Spondike
Price Range: Lunch/$5.95-$9.95
Dinner/$13.95-$23.95

Stuffed Carolina Quail

1 cup spinach, wilted in butter
4 ounces smoked Gouda cheese
6 oven-roasted shallots

4 semi-boneless quail
2 tablespoons extra virgin olive oil
½ cup seasoned flour

Combine first 3 ingredients. Divide mixture into four portions and stuff into body cavity of quail. Brush each bird, liberally, with extra virgin olive oil and lightly dredge in flour. In a hot pan, sear quail on both sides to achieve a golden crust. Transfer to a 425 degree oven and roast approximately 8 to 10 minutes or until firm to touch.

Yield: 2 servings

Chef's Suggestions: *Superb served upon a bed of garlic whipped potatoes, accompanied by your favorite sautéed vegetable. A rich sauce, incorporating red wine and reduced brown stock, provides the crowning touch for this dish.*

Restaurants
Charleston, South Carolina

Walnut Encrusted Stuffed Chicken

4 boneless, skinless chicken breasts
2 cloves fresh garlic, minced
1 cup yellow onion, diced
4 ounces smoked ham, diced
1 cup mushrooms, diced
1 stick unsalted butter
1 bunch fresh chives, chopped

2 tablespoons fresh parsley, chopped
1 cup dry white wine
1 cup heavy cream
1 cup flour
2 eggs, well beaten
2 cups walnuts, crushed

Using a meat mallet, pound chicken breasts to achieve uniform thickness; set aside. In a medium pan, sauté next 4 ingredients in butter. When onions become translucent, add next 4 ingredients and simmer, briefly, to reduce wine and further intensify flavors. Slowly incorporate flour and continue stirring until mixture thickens. Remove stuffing mixture from heat and set aside to cool.

Place a heaping tablespoon of stuffing on each chicken breast; roll breast, while tucking in the ends, to form a pocket. Using a standard breading technique, dredge breasts into flour, egg wash, and the crushed walnuts. Heat oil in a cast iron pan to approximately 350 degrees. Pan fry breasts on all sides to achieve a crisp, golden texture. Place in a 400 degree oven and continue cooking until done.

Yield: 4 servings

Chef's Suggestions: *Try serving this dish with rice or polenta. A simple cream sauce, flavored with chicken broth and a few mushrooms, makes a great addition.*

Editors' Notes: *The chicken breasts may be prepared, in advance, and refrigerated until time to cook them,*

"Poogan's Porch is about southern favorites, big portions, reasonable prices, and authentic charm.
--*The Post and Courier*

"Once you've tasted the food at Poogan's Porch, you'll understand why magazines like *Bon Appetit*, *Gourmet*, and *Cuisine* have requested their recipes."
--*TravelHost Magazine*

Long Point Inn

Overlooking a scenic marsh and next door to Boone Hall Plantation,
Long Point Inn offers a refreshing Lowcountry B & B experience.

Address: 1199 Long Point Road
Mount Pleasant, SC 29464
Telephone: (843)849-1884
E-mail: info@Charleston–
LongPtInn.com

Web Site: www.charleston–
longptinn.com
Category: B & B
Proprietress: Catharine Jennings
Rates: $89-$179 (seasonal)

Cheese-Laced Hash Browns

1 package of shredded hash browns
1 can cream of celery soup
8 ounces shredded Cheddar cheese

¾ cup sour cream
½ stick butter, melted
½-1 cup onion,

Spray (or grease with butter) a 2-quart glass baking dish. Combine all ingredients and spread in baking dish. Bake in a 350 degree oven for 45 minutes -
1 hour.

Yield: 8-10 servings

Editors' Note: *Add 1 pound of browned ground beef and top with additional cheese to create a main dish meal.*

Charleston Cheese Soufflé

3 cups fresh, untoasted white bread cubes
1 cup fresh or frozen chopped onion
Salt and pepper
12 ounces grated Cheddar cheese
1½ cups milk

4 eggs, beaten
1 tablespoon Worcestershire sauce
2 tablespoons yellow mustard
3 tomatoes, thinly sliced
3 tablespoons butter, sliced

Spray an 8½ x 11 inch glass baking dish with baking spray or grease with butter. Combine bread cubes, onion, salt and pepper, and 8 ounces of grated cheese. Spread into baking dish. Combine milk with next 3 ingredients; mix well. Pour egg mixture over ingredients in the baking dish and sprinkle with remaining cheese. Arrange tomato slices on top and dot with sliced butter. Bake in a 325 degree oven for 1 hour.

Yield: 6 servings

Editors' Note: *An egg substitute may be used instead of eggs, and the soufflé may be prepared in advance and refrigerated overnight. Delicious served with cured ham!*

"This Charleston inn is new among the old--nestled amongst a stand of 300 year old live oak trees, it is the perfect setting for a quality Bed and Breakfast right in the middle of one of the most historical sections in America." *--Gwinette Daily Post*

Long Point Inn, built upon historic property once part of Snee Farm Plantation and owned by Charles Pinckney (a signer of The Constitution), became part of Boone Hall Plantation after being sold to Governor Alexander Stone. The marsh front served as prosperous rice fields.

Price House Cottage

This National Register property lies in the heart of Summerville's Historic District

Address: 224 Sumter Avenue
Summerville, SC 29483
Telephone: (843)871-1877
E–mail: phcbb@aol.com

Web Site: www.bbonline.com/sc/
pricehouse/index.html
Category: B & B
Owners/Innkeepers: Jennifer & David Price
Rate: $145 (year-round)

Pumpkin Belgian Waffles with Vermont Maple Syrup Whipped Cream

(Adapted from *Morning Glories*, by Donna Leahy)

2 cups all-purpose flour
¼ cup sugar
4 teaspoons baking powder
1 teaspoon salt
1 teaspoon cinnamon
1 teaspoon ginger

¼ teaspoon cloves
1½ cups milk
1 cup pumpkin puree, canned
4 eggs, separated
1 cup butter, melted

Preheat waffle iron (Belgian or regular). In a large bowl, combine first 7 ingredients. Whisk together milk, pumpkin puree, and egg yolks. Stir pumpkin mixture into the dry ingredients and add melted butter. Beat egg whites until stiff and fold into pumpkin mixture. Ladle batter onto waffle iron and cook until steam ceases to escape from the iron, producing a lightly browned waffle.

Flavored Whipping Cream

1 cup whipping cream   2 tablespoons pure maple syrup

Whip the cream until peaks begin to appear. Add syrup, when peaks begin forming, and finish whipping the cream until stiff peaks form. Serve waffles with pure maple syrup and a generous scoop of the whipped cream.

Yield: 6

Editors' Notes: *Add chopped pecans to this batter and cook as pancakes-- ideal during the Thanksgiving season!*

Artichoke Baked Eggs

(Adapted from *The New Basics Cookbook* by Rosso and Lukins)

1 medium tomato,
  sliced ¼ inch thick, peeled and seeded
¼ teaspoon salt
2 tablespoons unsalted butter
8 ounces lean ham, cubed
2 tablespoons freshly grated
  Parmesan cheese

4 artichoke hearts, thinly
  sliced lengthwise. Use canned,
  but not marinated artichoke hearts.
3 tablespoons sour cream
4 eggs, separated
Freshly ground pepper to taste

Preheat oven to 450 degrees and place pot of water on stove to boil. Slice, peel, and seed tomato; place between paper towels to absorb moisture. Sauté ham in 1 tablespoon unsalted butter until slightly browned. Remove to paper towel to absorb any liquid.

Place half the ham in each of the bottoms of two oval 9 x 5 x 2-inch ramekins. Place tomato slices over ham to cover in single thickness. Sprinkle with Parmesan cheese and salt. Place the artichoke slices evenly over cheese and cover with sour cream. Spread sour cream evenly and place two indentations on each preparation with back of a spoon that has been run under hot water. Place the egg yolks in the indentations.

In a small bowl break up the egg whites with a fork so that they will flow as a liquid; do not beat the whites. Pour this mixture over the ramekins, being careful to keep the egg whites from running over the edge of the ramekins. Place ½ tablespoon of unsalted butter on top of each ramekin. Place the ramekins in a shallow roasting pan (or Pyrex baking dish) for a water bath. Fill with boiling water to reach approximately ⅔ the way up the ramekins.

Bake for 11 minutes. Remove from the water bath and place ramekins on individual plates. Sprinkle with freshly ground pepper and garnish with freshly chopped parsley. There will be a small amount of liquid on top of the ramekin at the end of cooking. This is melted butter and not uncooked egg.

Yield: 2 servings

One of the earliest houses in Summerville, the main house was built as a summer retreat from Charleston's heat and humidity. The cottage, a former servant's quarters at the rear of the property, is a past recipient of the Summerville Preservation Society Restoration Award.

Rice Hope Plantation

A 17th century rice plantation where time is still marked by the tides in the river

Address: 206 Rice Hope Drive
Moncks Corner, SC 29461
Reservations: 1-800-569-4038
Telephone: (843)761-4832
E-mail: lou@ricehope.com

Web Site: www.ricehope.com
Category: B & B
Proprietor: Lou Edens
Innkeepers: Jamie and Katie Edens
Rates: $85-$165

Rosebud Farms Fruit Dish

5-6 Golden Delicious apples
1 (16-ounce) can cranberry sauce (whole berries)
1 (8-ounce) can crushed pineapple, drained

Peel, core, and dice apples. Add cranberry sauce and pineapple.
Pour into a 9 x 13-inch baking dish; cover and refrigerate overnight.
Bring to room temperature.

Topping

¼ cup flour
⅓ cup brown sugar
½ cup raw oatmeal

½ teaspoon cinnamon
¼ cup butter

Mix all topping ingredients and sprinkle on top of fruit. Bake at 350
degrees for 45 minutes. Serve hot or cold.

Yield: 8 servings

ଔ-ଔ

Sunrise Pleaser

2 pounds sausage, cooked & drained
½ pound grated cheese
4 eggs, beaten
1 cup cooked grits
1 (6-ounce) package cornbread mix
1 ½ cups milk, heated
½ cup butter, melted
¾ teaspoon salt

Grease 9 x 13-inch baking dish. Layer sausage and half of the cheese on bottom of dish. Mix eggs and next 5 ingredients. Pour over sausage mixture and top with remaining cheese. Refrigerate overnight. Bring to room temperature. Bake at 350 degrees for 45 to 60 minutes. Check center for doneness with a toothpick.

Yield: 4 servings

Editors' Note: *Broiled tomatoes are an excellent side dish for this delicious breakfast or brunch casserole.*

Selected for *"Best Places to Stay Guides"*

_____

The original house burned and was rebuilt in 1840. The present 40-room mansion is the result of renovations and additions made in 1929 by U.S. Senator John S. Frelinghugsen of New Jersey who used the property as a hunting lodge.

The formal gardens (est. 1795) were restored and enhanced in the 1930's according to a design by noted landscape architect Loutrell Briggs.

Woodlands Resort & Inn

A 1906 Greek Revival mansion impeccably restored in the best English tradition

Address: 125 Parsons Road
Summerville, SC 29483
Reservations: 1-800-774-9999
Telephone: (843)875-2600
E-mail: reservations@woodlandsinn.com

Web Site: www.woodlandsinn.com
Category: An Historic Inn
Proprietor: Marty Wall
Rates: $295-$395

Woodlands Tea Scones with Berries and Sweet Cream

2 cups flour
½ teaspoon salt
1 tablespoon black pepper
¼ cup butter
1 egg

½ cup milk
1 pint crème fraîche (sweet cream)
Fresh seasonal berries
Egg wash
Sugar

Sift dry ingredients, crumb in butter. Make a well in center of mixture and add beaten egg and milk. The dough must be sticky (add more milk, if needed). Scrape dough mixture into plastic wrap and pat out into a block. Refrigerate until cold and punch into desired shapes. Brush with egg wash and roll in sugar before baking at 400 degrees for 10 minutes. Serve with sweet cream and berries.

Yield: 12 scones

Croissant French Toast
with Huckleberries and Maple Syrup Ice-Cream

1 bottle Elysium (a California dessert wine)	4 eggs
½ cup sugar	½ cup cream
1 tablespoon orange peel scrapings	1 teaspoon vanilla extract
1 cinnamon stick	4 stale croissants, bottom & tops cut off
1 cup fresh blueberries	1 cup corn flakes, crushed
(or Huckleberry's frozen blueberries)	4 scoops of favorite ice-cream

Add bottle of Elysium to pan and cook to burn off alcohol. Add next 3 ingredients. Cook down until mixture coats back of a spoon; add berries and keep warm.

Mix eggs, cream, and vanilla together. Soak croissant slices for almost 1 minute; turning over once. Dip each side of croissant slices into crushed corn flakes. Place on a greased cookie sheet and bake at 325 degrees for 10 minutes. Place croissant slices on a plate and top with a scoop of ice-cream. Spoon berries over top of ice cream.

Yield: 4 servings

Editors' Note: *If you do not have a favorite ice cream flavor, try one of the variations on page 124.*

"Outstanding--worth a special trip"
-- *Mobil Travel Guide*

"Among the top ten hotels for service in the world."
--*Conde Nast Traveler,* January 2002

"A 30-minute drive from Charleston, Woodlands is one of the finest places to stay in the Lowcountry." --*Frommer's Guide*

"Gracious without being overly grand, the Woodlands is the kind of civilized retreat that should be at the heart of any visit to town or country." --*Town & Country Magazine, John Cantrell (March 2001)*

Oscar's

Quite simply fine dining at its best

Address: 207 W. 5th Street North
Summerville, SC 29483
Telephone: (843)871-3800

Cuisine: American Eclectic
Executive Chef: David Langenstein
Price Range: $8-$24

Bananas Oscar

1 ripe banana,
   sliced lengthwise and halved
4 tablespoons rum (light)
4 tablespoons banana liqueur
4 tablespoons brown sugar

3 tablespoon butter
4 scoops vanilla ice 7cream
4 tablespoons candied pecans*
Whipped Cream, optional
Chopped pecans, optional

Combine rum and next 3 ingredients in a sauté pan over medium heat. Bring to a simmer and add sliced banana; cook briefly on each side. Keep warm.

* Candied Pecans

2 ounces melted butter   1 pound pecan pieces   4 ounces brown sugar

Combine all ingredients, spread evenly on a baking sheet, and bake at 450 degrees for ten minutes. Remove and cool. Save extra pecans for next time or for delicious snacking.

Place 2 scoops of ice-cream in bowl with candied pecans and toss to coat. Place ice-cream in a bowl. Pour bananas and sauce over ice-cream. Garnish with whipped cream and more pecans, if desired.

Yield: 2 servings

Editors' Note: *Prepare candied pecans in advance and roll ice-cream scoops in pecans. Place 2 scoops into individual banana split dishes and place in freezer until ready to use.*

❧❧❧❧❧❧❧❧❧❧❧❧❧❧❧❧❧❧❧❧❧❧❧❧❧

Horseradish Encrusted Deep Fried Oysters, Stuffed with Brie wrapped in Apple-smoked Bacon, Champagne Sauce, and Sweet Onion Marmalade

½ cup freshly grated horseradish
2 cups bread crumbs
½ tablespoon fresh basil
1 tablespoon freshly chopped parsley
½ cup milk
3 eggs, beaten
2 cups flour

Salt and pepper to taste
Old Bay seasoning to taste
18 large select oysters
6 ounces Brie
6 slices apple-smoked bacon, cut into thirds
18 toothpicks
2 cups mesclun greens for garnish

Heat Fryer 350 degrees. Mix horseradish and next 3 ingredients together until blended. Add milk to beaten eggs in a separate bowl. Season flour with salt, pepper, and Old Bay seasoning. Cut a slit into side of each oyster; stuff with Brie, wrap with bacon, and skewer with a toothpick. Dredge stuffed oyster in flour, dip then in egg mixture, and coat with bread crumbs. Deep fry oysters until golden brown, removing toothpicks when done. Serve with Champagne Sauce* and Onion Marmalade.**

*Champagne Sauce

3 ounces champagne
1 teaspoon shallots
1½ cups heavy cream

6 ounces butter
Parsley

Add champagne and shallots to sauce pan; reduce by half. Add cream, reduce by one-half. Whip in butter. Garnish with parsley.

**Onion Marmalade

1 jumbo onion (sliced)
2 ounces apple cider vinegar
1 ounce white sugar
1 ounce brown sugar

2 ounce dry sherry
Salt and pepper to taste

Heat heavy sauté pan. Add onion and cook until brown. Add next 4 ingredients and cook until dry. Add salt and pepper

Yield: 6 servings

Considered "a restaurant worth repeating" among locals since 1982.

Seewee Restaurant

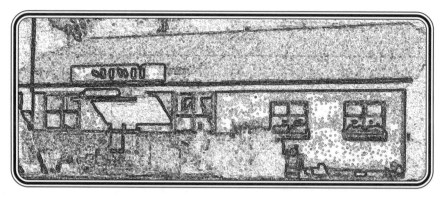

A general store turned into a restaurant serving homemade specialties.

Address: 4808 Highway 17N
Awendaw, SC 29429
(north of Charleston)

Telephone: (843)928-3609
Cuisine: Southern style cooking & seafood
Price Range: $8.95-$19.95

Mary's Okra Soup

1 meaty ham bone
4 cups red ripe tomatoes, cored and chopped
  (may substitute 4 cups tomato purée or 4 cups canned tomatoes, undrained)
4 cups fresh okra, cut--or 2 (6-ounce packages) frozen okra may be substituted
Salt and pepper to taste

Place ham bone in 4 cups of boiling water. Lower heat and continue cooking until meat falls off bone. Add tomatoes (or purée) and cook for about an hour. Add okra last, season with salt and pepper, and cook on low heat until tender (about thirty minutes).

Yield: 6-8 servings

Contributor's Note: For a good vegetable soup, add desired amount of fresh or frozen green lima beans and corn. Add beans with tomatoes and add corn with okra. Cook an additional hour.

Editors' Note: *Instead of using a ham bone, brown 1 pound of ground chuck in a Dutch oven, breaking up with a metal spatula. Add 4 cups of water, tomatoes, okra, and season to taste. Before serving, sprinkle soup with grated Parmesan or Cheddar cheese. Extra good with additional vegetables (petite lima beans and shoepeg white corn) added.*

Lowcountry Boil

3 pounds small white potatoes
Salt and pepper to taste
Old Bay seasoning to taste
1 whole sliced lemon
3 garlic cloves

3 pounds Hillshire Sausage,
   cut in 1-inch slices
5 pound bag corn-on-the-cob,
   fresh or frozen
5 pounds shrimp, shells on
3 dozen small clams in shell

Put potatoes and seasonings in pot with enough water to cover; simmer until almost done. Add sausage and corn; cook until done. Add clams and shrimp; cook until pink. Serve hot.

Yield: 15 servings

Editors' Note: *Along the South Carolina/Georgia coast, a Lowcountry Boil is more than a popular meal, it is an event steeped in Lowcountry tradition. The classic coastal dish, sometimes referred to as Frogmore Stew, offers diners a variety of culinary choices in one big pot. It is served in a casual outdoor setting.*

Recommended by *1st Traveler's Choice.*

Recommended as one of the "top choices" for lowcountry cuisine by travel writer Lynn Seldon, *New York Post.*

Listed as one of South Carolina's Secrets in
100 Secrets of the Carolina Coast,
by Randall H. Duckett and Maryellen K. Duckett

Trawler Seafood Restaurant

Its waterside location provides an authentic ambience in a relaxed setting.

Address: 100 Church Street
Mt. Pleasant, SC 29464
Telephone: (843) 884-2560
Web Site: www.thetrawler.com

Cuisine: Specializing in seafood
Executive Chef: Michael Rogers
Price Range: Lunch/$5-$13
Dinner/$13-$27

Crab Dip

1 pound crabmeat
1 tablespoon Worcestershire sauce
½ teaspoon Tabasco sauce
1 ounce chili sauce

2 ounces Cheddar cheese
½ teaspoon lemon Juice
½ teaspoon prepared horseradish
½ cup mayonnaise (more if needed)

Mix all ingredients together; let sit for one hour to absorb flavors.
Serve cold with crackers or toast points.

Yield: 8-10 servings

Editors' Note: *Make sure enough mayonnaise is added to enable crab to stick together when spreading.*

Fruit de Mer Crowned with Brandied Lobster Sauce

Lobster Stock

¼ cup olive oil
2½ pounds lobster cavities,
   chopped into 2-inch pieces
½ yellow onion, diced
2 stalks celery, diced
½ leek (white only), diced
½ medium carrot, cleaned and diced
3 teaspoons parsley

½ teaspoon fresh tarragon
1 bay leaf
1 black peppercorn
2½ teaspoons white pepper
1 tomato, diced
½ small can tomato paste
1½ gallons water
1 cup brandy

Heat olive oil up in a stock pot. Add lobster bodies and sauté until bright red; add next 4 ingredients and sauté until soft. Add herbs, peppercorns, diced tomatoes, and tomato paste. Sauté mixture until thoroughly incorporated; deglaze with brandy. Slowly add water to stock pot and bring to a simmer. Cook for 1½ hours or until liquid has reduced by 25%. Strain liquid and put aside.

Lobster Sauce

¼ pound butter
½ cup shallots, diced
½ cup garlic, diced
½ cup brandy

1 cup all-purpose flour, sifted
Lobster stock (from recipe)
½ quart heavy cream, 36% milk fat
Salt and white pepper to taste

Melt butter in stock pot and add shallots and garlic; sauté until translucent. Deglaze with brandy and slowly add flour to pan to create a roux. Add enough flour so that a spoon cleans bottom of pan. Cook roux until proper consistency is achieved over low heat. Slowly add stock in 4 parts to ensure no roux balls form. Bring to a simmer to cook out roux and add heavy cream. Check seasoning to ensure proper flavor has been achieved. Strain liquid through china cap to get rid of any by-product. Hold.

Fruit de Mer

¾ pound shrimp
¾ pound scallops
½ pound crab meat
2 teaspoons garlic
1 leek, white only

3 tomatoes (dice and save one for garnish)
2 ounces basil (half for sauce, half for plate)
1 cup cream
3 pounds cooked linguine, drained

Sauté first seven ingredients in olive oil; add cream and lobster sauce. Put hot pasta on plates (or in bowls), ladle sauce and seafood over top, garnish with diced tomato and basil.

Yield: 12 servings

The Trawler Restaurant has been serving seafood to The Lowcountry for over 35 years.

Woodlands Dining Room

Woodland's Dining Room, the only AAA Five Diamond award-winning dining room in South Carolina, enjoys a stellar reputation from food critics around the world.

Address: 125 Parsons Road
Summerville, SC 29483
Telephone: (843)875-2600
Web Site: www.woodlandsinn.com/
restaurant.htm

Cuisine: New American
Executive Chef: KenVedrinski
Price Range: $59 (A la carte menu)
$120 ("Tasting" menu)
$120 (Chef's Table in
the kitchen)

Butternut Squash Soup

3 strips smoked bacon
1 large sweet onion, chopped
3 stalks celery, peeled and chopped
1 large butternut squash, peeled, seeded,
diced and cubed into 1-inch cubes
4 cups chicken stock (may use canned)

1 cup crème fraîche or whipping cream
Salt to taste
White pepper to taste
2 tablespoons of organic honey
1 leek (white part only), chopped

Sauté bacon, sweet onion, and celery. Add butternut squash and chicken stock. Simmer until squash is soft; add next 5 ingredients and blend together. Pass through a strainer. Garnish with chives and pancetta or smoked duck.

Yield: 4-6 servings

Editors' Note: *An excellent soup to serve during the fall months when butternut squash is in season.*

Hot Smoked Maine Salmon with Curry Oil

½ pound salt
½ pound sugar
1 tablespoon crushed black pepper
12 pieces of salmon (no bones, skin, or fat)
Applewood (for grilling)

Mix salt, sugar and pepper. Pack around salmon until completely covered. Let sit for 1 hour at room temperature.

Marinade	*Curry Oil*
1 cup apple cider	1 teaspoon curry powder
1 tablespoon fresh dill, chopped	¼ cup grapeseed (or safflower) oil
1 teaspoon mustard seeds	

Cook cider until reduced to syrup consistency; add dill and mustard seeds. Wash salt off salmon and cover with a thin layer of marinade. Combine grapeseed oil and curry powder; let sit for 3 hours.

Light applewood* over fire until a good burn develops. Put in oven at 250 degrees for 16 to 20 minutes. Let cool for 2 hours; pour curry oil around grilled salmon.

Yield: 12 servings

Editors' note: *Applewood is used for flavoring in the cooking process. Soak wood in water and place on top of heat source (grill or wood oven). Hickory or mesquite wood may be substituted.*

"The only perfect food score in North America."
-- Gold List/2002 *Reader's Choice Awards*

Conde Nast Traveler's 2000 Reader Poll named
The Dining Room at Woodlands
"one of the top three restaurants in North America."

A white-pillared Classical Revival building, originally constructed in 1906, Woodlands stands on 42 landscaped acres.

"The most beautiful city in North America" --*Le Monde*

※ ※ ※ ※ ※ ※ ※ ※ ※ ※ ※ ※ ※ ※ ※ ※ ※

One of the "Top 12 Trendy Hot Spots in the World" --*New York Times*

※ ※ ※ ※ ※ ※ ※ ※ ※ ※ ※ ※ ※ ※ ※ ※ ※

One of "America's Top 10 U. S. Cities to Visit" --*Conde Nast Traveler*

※ ※ ※ ※ ※ ※ ※ ※ ※ ※ ※ ※ ※ ※ ※ ※

One of "Top 200 places in the Country" --*Forbes Magazine*

※ ※ ※ ※ ※ ※ ※ ※ ※ ※ ※ ※ ※ ※ ※ ※

One of "Top 10 Southeast Cities for Family Vacations" --*Family Fun Magazine*

※ ※ ※ ※ ※ ※ ※ ※ ※ ※ ※ ※ ※ ※ ※ ※

"The stretch of coast from Savannah southward is...the most beautiful place in the world."   --Margaret Mitchell, author of *Gone With the Wind*

※ ※ ※ ※ ※ ※ ※ ※ ※ ※ ※ ※ ※ ※ ※ ※

Welcome to Savannah, the sultry and mysterious "Belle" of the Southeastern coast. Savannah captivates the suitors that come to call with her natural beauty, eccentric charm and traditional Southern Hospitality — because Savannah is genteel, gracious and captivating. Savannah is the beautifully preserved hidden treasure of the Low Country. Come unlock the history, romance and beauty that lies within. Explore every nook and cranny because you are her guest and Savannah loves sharing her treasures with you.

Web Site for Savannah, GA
www.savannahvisit.com

Savannah
"Soul of the South"

Original artwork by Theron Wallis

Picturesque Johnson Square is a magical place to savor Savannah

Eliza Thompson House

Southern hospitality and romantic elegance for discriminating travelers

Address: 5 West Jones Street
Savannah, GA 31401
(Historic District)
Reservations: 1-800-348-9378
Telephone: (912)236-3620

Web Site: www.elizathompsonhouse.com
Category: An Historic Inn
Innkeeper: Jean Bearden
Rates: $119-$250 (seasonal)

Miss Virginia's Peach and Pecan Dip

8 ounces cream cheese
4 ounces peach preserves
1 cup chopped pecans

In a small food processor, blend the cream cheese until smooth. Add the peach preserves and mix well. Fold in the chopped pecans, reserving a teaspoonful to sprinkle on top. Refrigerate for at least 2 hours before serving. Serve chilled or at room temperature with your favorite crackers or toasted bread rounds.

Yield: 10-12 servings

Editors' Note: *This dip also makes a nice topping for small open-faced sandwiches on a party tray.*

〜〜〜〜〜〜〜〜〜〜〜〜〜〜〜〜〜〜〜〜〜〜〜〜〜〜

Salsa Egg Casserole

1 (16-ounce) jar mild salsa
2 cups shredded Cheddar cheese
12 eggs

1 (4-ounce) can chopped green chilies
3½ cups milk

Preheat oven to 350 degrees. Grease a 9 X 13-inch glass baking dish. Spread salsa on bottom of dish. Sprinkle cheddar cheese evenly over the salsa. Mix together the next 3 ingredients and pour mixture over cheese. Bake at 350 degrees for 40 to 50 minutes, or until eggs are firm.

Yield: 16-18 servings

The Eliza Thompson House, a Federal style three-story mansion is one of the oldest bed and breakfast inns in Savannah. Built for Eliza Thompson in 1847, the landmark recalls a prosperous time in Savannah where elegant parties in fine homes were popular.

The Foley House Inn

A unique combination of Southern hospitality and European charm

Address: 14 W. Hull Street
Savannah, GA 31401
(Historic District)
Reservations: 1-800-647-3708
Local Telephone: (912)232-6622

Web Site: www.foleyinn.com
Category: An Historic Inn
Owners/Innkeepers:
Beryl and Donald Zerwer
Rates: $195-$345

Southern Peach Crisp

1 cup flour
½ cup sugar
½ cup light brown sugar
¼ teaspoon salt
½ teaspoon ground cinnamon

½ cup salted butter
4 cups fresh peaches, sliced
1 tablespoon lemon juice
2 tablespoons water

Combine the first 5 ingredients. Cut in butter, until mixture resembles coarse corn meal. Combine last 3 ingredients and spoon into a greased 9 x 9 x 1¾-inch baking dish, preferably glass. Sprinkle flour mixture over peaches. Bake covered at 30 degrees for 15 minutes. Remove cover and bake an additional 35 to 45 minutes.

Yield: 4-6 servings

Cheese Blintzes

Batter

1 cup milk	¼ cup sugar
1 cup flour	1 teaspoon vanilla
1 tablespoon sour cream	Pinch salt
4 eggs	Cooking oil

Combine first 3 ingredients, blending well. Add eggs, 1 at a time, mixing until batter is smooth. Stir in next 3 ingredients. Heat a small amount of oil over a low flame in a frying pan until hot, but not smoking. Ladle a small portion of batter into pan, tipping pan in all directions until batter covers entire bottom of the pan. Fry on one side until set and golden, approximately 1 minute. Slip crêpe out of pan and repeat until all batter is used. Add small amounts of oil to the pan, if needed.

Filling

1 pound cottage cheese	1 tablespoon sugar
1 (8-ounce) package cream cheese	1 teaspoon vanilla
2 egg yolks	

Mix all ingredients for the filling and put aside.

Assembly

Fill each crepe on the golden side with approximately 3 tablespoons of filling. Fold outsides to center, rolling blintz until completely closed. Place rolled blintzes in a pan and fry for about 2 minutes, turning once. When ready to serve, place in a 350 degree oven for about 20 minutes, fry on top of stove for 2 minutes. Turn over. Ladle coulis over blintzes.

Coulis

1 cup cherries (pitted), blueberries, or raspberries	1 teaspoon lemon juice
1 cup water	2 tablespoons cornstarch, dissolved in water
½ cup sugar	

Boil fruit and water for 3 minutes. Over medium heat, stirring constantly, add sugar and lemon juice. Bring mixture back to a boil and slowly stir in the dissolved cornstarch mixture. Boil 1 minute to thicken.

Serves: 2

Rated one of ten "Most Romantic Inns" in the country
by *Vacation Magazine.*

Named By *Discovering Traveler*
as a Top "Romantic Hideaway of 1999"

Forsyth Park Inn

*Built in circa 1890, this Queen Anne Victorian mansion
overlooks Savannah's largest and most opulent park*

Address: 102 W. Hall Street
Savannah, GA 31401
(Historic District)
Reservations: 1-800-484-6850
Telephone: (912)233-6800

Web Site: www.forsythparkinn.com
Category: An Historic Inn
Owners/Innkeepers:
Lori & Richard Blass
Rates: $115-$230 (seasonal)

Fresh Fruit with Honey Yogurt Dip

2 cups vanilla yogurt
½ cup honey
1 teaspoon ground cinnamon

Assorted fresh fruit
(apples, bananas, pineapple, strawberries, etc.)
cut into wedges or bite-size pieces

Combine yogurt, honey, and cinnamon in small bowl; stir to blend. Place bowl on platter. Surround with fresh fruit and serve.

Yield: 2 cups of dip

Editors' Note: *A refreshing dip anytime, but especially when fresh fruits are in season.*

Bed & Breakfasts and Historic Inns
Savannah, Georgia

❧❧❧❧❧❧❧❧❧❧❧❧❧❧❧❧❧❧❧❧❧❧❧❧

Best-Ever Orange Sponge Cake

6 egg whites (¾ cup)	Confectioners' sugar
6 egg yolks	1½ cups granulated sugar
1¾ sifted all-purpose flour, divided	¼ teaspoon salt
1 tablespoon freshly grated orange peel	6 tablespoons fresh orange juice

In large bowl of electric mixer, let egg whites warm to room temperature (about 1 hour). Sift about 2 cups of flour onto a sheet of waxed paper; fill cups to slightly overflowing and level with spatula to make 1¾ level cups. Sift flour again with salt. Set aside. With electric mixer at medium speed, beat egg whites until foamy. Gradually beat in ½ cup of the granulated sugar, 2 tablespoons at a time, beating well after each addition. Continue beating until stiff peaks form when beaters are slowly raised. Set aside. Preheat oven to 350 degrees.

In small bowl of electric mixer, with the same beaters at high speed, beat egg yolks until thick and lemon-colored (about 3 minutes). Do not underbeat. Gradually beat in remaining 1 cup granulated sugar, and continue beating until mixture is smooth. At low speed, blend flour mixture and orange juice, alternately, into egg yolk mixture; begin and end with flour, guiding batter into beaters with scraper. Add orange peel. With a whisk or rubber spatula, using an under-and-over motion, fold yolk mixture gently into whites.

Pour batter into an ungreased 9¾-10 by 4½-inch kugelhopf or tube pan (one without a removable bottom). Bake 50 to 55 minutes in kugelhopf or 35 to 40 minutes in tube pan, until cake springs back when pressed with finger. Invert over a bottle. If using tube pan, invert cake onto a plate. Cool completely. Using an up-and-down motion, run spatula around the edge of cake and tube. Invert cake and shake to release. Place on serving plate or cake stand. Sift confectioners' sugar over top of cake. To cut cake, use a knife with serrated edge. Cut gently, going back and forth with sawing motion.

Yield: 1 cake

An elegant mansion restored to create the pampered lifestyle
of the nineteenth century.

The Gastonian

The only Relais & Chateaux property in Georgia, The Gastonian is known all over the world for its legendary hospitality and historic elegance

Address: 220 E. Gaston Street
Savannah, GA 31401
(Historic District)
Reservations: 1-800-322-6603
Telephone: (912)232-2869

Web Site: www.gastonian.com
Category: An Historic Inn
Owner/Innkeeper: Anne Landers
Rates: $250-$425

Lemon Ricotta Cheese Pancakes

1 cup all-purpose flour
2 tablespoons sugar
4 teaspoons baking powder
½ teaspoon salt

4 teaspoons lemon juice
2 cups part skim milk ricotta cheese
6 eggs, separated
¼ cup corn oil

Combine first 4 ingredients in the bowl of an electric mixer. Stir in next 2 ingredients until smooth. Beat in remaining ingredients until smooth. Whisk or beat egg whites until stiff peaks form; set aside. Beat eggs yolks and oil into flour mixture. Fold eggs whites into batter after all ingredients are combined. Stir until smooth.

Heat a lightly greased griddle (or skillet) over medium-high heat. Ladle batter onto griddle to form 3-4 inch cakes. Cook until small bubbles form and the edges begin browning, 2 to 3 minutes. Turn cakes and continue cooking 1 to 2 minutes longer, until just cooked through. Repeat procedure until all batter is used.

Yield: 12 pancakes

Bed & Breakfasts and Historic Inns
Savannah, Georgia

ഗ‐ഗ‐ഗ‐ഗ‐ഗ‐ഗ‐ഗ‐ഗ‐ഗ‐ഗ‐ഗ‐ഗ‐ഗ‐ഗ‐ഗ‐ഗ‐ഗ‐ഗ‐ഗ‐ഗ

Vidalia Onion Bites

1 cup mayonnaise
1 cup Parmesan cheese
1 Vidalia onion, finely chopped

Sliced bread, crust removed
(white or wheat seem
to work best)

Mix all ingredients and spread onto bread. Cut into bite-size pieces and bake at 375 degrees for approximately 10 minutes or until light brown.

Yield: About 3 dozen servings

Editors' Note: *An easy and delicious hors d'oeuvre using Georgia's famous Vidalia onions.*

Ham Bites

1 cup fine, dry breadcrumbs, divided
1 cup ground cooked ham
2 eggs, beaten
½ cup (2-ounces) shredded sharp Cheddar cheese

¼ cup grated onion
2 tablespoons brown sugar
1 tablespoon Dijon mustard

Combine ½ cup of bread crumbs with remaining ingredients in a large bowl Stir well. Shape ham mixture into 1-inch balls and roll into remaining ½ cup bread crumbs, pressing firmly so crumbs adhere. Cover and chill for 30 minutes. Next place ham bites onto a lightly greased baking sheet and bake for 10 minutes at 360 degrees. You may also deep-fry these bites for 2 minutes in vegetable oil, if desired.

Yield: 2½ dozen

"...one of the best inns in the United States." --*The Andrew Harper Report*

"...the Grand Dame of Savannah inns." --*Great Country Inns*

"...The most famous of Savannah inns and justifiably so."
-- *The New York Times*

"...one of the 12 most romantic inns on the East Coast."
--*The Discerning Traveler*

"...An elite and immaculate small hotel." --*Johannsens Guide to the USA*

Granite Steps

Voted Savannah's Most Romantic Bed and Breakfast Inn

Address: 126 E. Gaston Street
Savannah, GA 31401
(Historic District)
Telephone: (912)233-5380

WebSite: www.granitesteps.com
Category: An Historic Inn
Owner/Innkeeper: Donna Sparks
Price Range: $250-$500 (seasonal)

Artichoke Dip

1 (16-ounce) can artichoke hearts, drained
1 cup mayonnaise
1 tablespoon lemon juice

Tabasco sauce to taste
1 cup grated Parmesan cheese
1 bag tortilla chips

Preheat oven to 350 degrees. Place artichokes in bowl of food processor and process until roughly chopped. Add remaining ingredients and mix well. Bake for 10 minutes or until bubbly. Serve with tortilla chips.

Yield: 6 servings

Editors' Note: *Just as good when reheated.*

Berry Good French Toast Bake

½ cup flour
1½ cups milk
1 tablespoon sugar
½ teaspoon vanilla
¼ teaspoon salt
1 teaspoon cinnamon
½ teaspoon nutmeg

6 eggs
10 slices (1-inch thick) French bread,
    cut into 1 inch cubes
3-ounces cream cheese,
    cut into ½ inch cubes.
1 cup fresh or frozen blueberries
½ cup chopped pecans

Generously grease a 1 (13x 9-inch) pan or baking dish. Beat first 8 ingredients in a large bowl with hand beater until smooth. Stir in bread cubes until coated. Pour bread mixture into pan, topping evenly with remaining ingredients. Cover and refrigerate up to 24 hours. Heat oven to 400 degrees. Uncover dish and bake 20 to 25 minutes, or until golden brown. Drizzle with melted butter and sprinkle with powdered sugar. Serve with syrup, if desired.

Yield: 8 servings

Voted Savannah's #1 Inn by *TravelHost* Magazine.
September 2001

*Selected as a site for a scene in Clint Eastwood's film version
of the New York Times best seller*
Midnight in the Garden of Good and Evil.

Hamilton Turner Inn

A grand Victorian mansion overlooking beautiful Lafayette Square

Address: 330 Abercorn Street
Savannah, GA 31401
(Historic District)
Reservations: 1-888-448-8849
Telephone: (912)233-1833

Category: An Historic Inn
Owners/Innkeepers:
Sue and Charlie Strickland
Price Range: $169-$500
Web Site: www.hamilton-turnerinn.com

Ashley's Scottish Shortbread

2 cups butter, softened
1⅔ cups sugar
4 cups all-purpose flour

1⅓ cups cornstarch
sugar for sprinkling

Cream the butter and sugar until fluffy. In a separate bowl, mix the flour and cornstarch. Slowly add the flour mixture to the butter and sugar until blended. Using a cookie sheet topped with baking paper, roll out the dough to a 1 inch thickness. Bake at 350 degrees for 30 minutes or until lightly brown. Remove from the oven and sprinkle with sugar on top while still warm. Cut into lengths approximately 1x3 inches. Can be stored in an airtight container for up to 1 week.

Editors' Note: *The best shortbread we've tasted outside of Edinburgh!*

କରୋକରୋକରୋକରୋକରୋକରୋକରୋକରୋକରୋକରୋକରୋକରୋକରୋକରୋକରୋ

Charlie's Dutch Apple Pancake

2 tablespoons butter
6 tablespoons sugar

3 large apples (peeled, halved, cored, and sliced)
1 tablespoons cinnamon

Melt the butter in a large frying pan on the stove. Add the sugar, apples, cinnamon, and sauté ¾, stirring continuously until the apples are soft. Transfer the apples to a 9x12-inch oven-proof dish.

3 eggs
½ cup all purpose flour
½ cup milk
1 tablespoons sour cream

⅛ teaspoon salt
½ teaspoon grated lemon zest
powdered sugar for topping

Using an electric mixer, beat the eggs until whipped. Add the flour, milk, sour cream, salt, and lemon zest and mix until blended. Pour the pancake mixture over the apples. Bake at 400 degrees for 25 minutes or until puffy and firm in the center. Cut into squares. Sprinkle with powdered sugar.

Yield: 10 servings

"For a true Southern breakfast to authentic afternoon tea
service, all guests enjoy these homemade delights."
-- *TravelHost spotlight, 1998*

The President's Quarters

An Inn of distinction harboring Savannah history—a place in time where diplomats, generals, and governors planned and influenced Savannah's history.

Address: 225 E. President Street
Savannah, Georgia 31401
(Historic District)
Reservations: 1-800-233-1776
Telephone: (912)233-1600

Website: www.presidentsquarters.com
Category: An Historic Inn
Owners/Innkeepers: Stacy Stephens
and Hank Smalling
Rates: $137-$250

Crabby Caps

1 (8-ounce) package cream cheese
1 pound crab meat
2 tablespoons mayonnaise
Pinch of dill

Dash of liquid smoke
2 pints white button mushrooms
Melted butter
Parsley or chives

Soften cream cheese; combine next four ingredients. Remove stems from mushroom caps. Brush caps with a light coating of melted butter. Fill caps with crab mixture. Bake for 15 minutes at 375 degrees. Garnish with parsley or chives.

Yield: 20 appetizer servings

Apple Krispin' Bread

1 egg	1 teaspoon baking soda
½ cup corn oil	½ teaspoon baking powder
½ cup milk (2%)	¼ teaspoon salt
1 cup sugar	2 cups diced apples,
1 teaspoon vanilla	(Granny Smith type)
2½ cups sifted white flour	

Topping

1 cup brown sugar	⅓ cup chopped nuts
2 tablespoons flour	(either walnuts, hazelnuts,
1 teaspoon cinnamon	or pecans)

Set oven to bake at 350 degrees. Beat together first 5 ingredients. Add next five ingredients and mix, lightly, until lumpy. Mix topping in separate bowl. Pour mixture into a prepared loaf pan (buttered, oiled, or sprayed) and crumble 2-3 tablespoons of topping over dough. Bake for 45 minutes or until top is firm (check the middle, with a toothpick, for doneness). To moisten bread, freeze overnight before eating. Keep extra topping in the refrigerator for next time.

Yield: 15-20 servings

"Gracious living indeed!
And the staff are genuinely friendly and interested."
-- Terry Houston, *The London Herald*

"When you go back and stay a fourth or fifth time, it's like staying in a friend's house. They value the relationship they have with you."
-- JoBeth McDaniel, *Working Women*

Located on Oglethorpe Square, these twin Federal style townhouses were built in 1855 under the auspices of the W. W. Gordon (grandfather of Juliette Gordon Lowe) Estate. It is across the street from The Owens-Thomas house, famous for its Regency architecture and the balcony from which Marquis de Lafayette once presented a speech during a visit to Savannah.

William Kehoe House

A stately Renaissance Revival mansion overlooking Columbia Square

Address: 123 Habersham Street
Savannah, GA 31401
(Historic District)
Reservations: 1-800-820-1020
Telephone: (912)232-1020

Category: An Historic Inn
Price Range: $205-$295 (seasonal)
Web Site: www.williamkehoehouse.com
Note: *The Kehoe House was renamed
The William Kehoe House in February 2001
under new ownership and management*

Chocolate Chip Praline Pecan Pie

3 eggs
½ cup sugar
¼ cup sifted cornstarch
2 ounces praline liqueur

1 cup chopped pecans
1 cup chocolate chips
4 ounces melted butter
1 (9-inch) unbaked pie shell

Preheat oven to 350 degrees. Add all ingredients together and mix well. Pour into the unbaked pie shell and bake for 50 to 60 minutes. Filling may appear to be under-cooked, but it will not be. Do not refrigerate the pie.

Yield: 6-8 servings

Editors' Note: *Walnuts may be substituted for pecans, if desired. Good topped with whipped cream flavored with more praline liqueur.*

Sweet Potato Pecan Pancakes

3 cups white flour
1 cup wheat flour
4 teaspoons baking powder
1 teaspoon baking soda
2 teaspoons cinnamon
½ teaspoon ginger
¾ cup chopped pecans
6 eggs

2 tablespoons orange zest (rind)
4 cups buttermilk
⅓ cup canola oil
3½ cups peeled, boiled,
    mashed sweet potato
    (or same amount canned)
4 tablespoons brown sugar
2 teaspoons vanilla

In large bowl stir together first 7 ingredients. In a separate bowl combine remaining ingredients. Add to dry ingredients and stir just until well-mixed. Pour batter onto a hot griddle by one-third cup measure (may need to be smoothed-out a bit). Cook until slightly browned. Serve with ginger butter.

Yield: 24 pancakes (serves 8-12)

Ginger Butter

1 cup soft butter
3 tablespoons finely chopped candied ginger

Mix together until well-blended.

"Total Southern elegance enhanced by a hospitable, knowledgeable staff."
-- Jim Kott, *America's Favorite Inns, B & B's, and Small Hotels*

"An eclectic mix of styles makes this distinctive brick house one of Savannah's finest mansions and an outstanding inn in a city known for its historic guest houses." -- *Georgia Journal*, 1997

"In a city characterized by grand homes and beautiful inns, The Kehoe House distinguishes itself as a delightful combination of the two."
-- *Best Read Guide* Savannah, August 1999

"Elegant and expert at pampering guests, the Kehoe House is all you could hope for in a B & B and more."-- *Points North*, October 2000

17 Hundred 90

Captures the authentic flavor of Georgia's first and most romantic city

Address: 307 E. President St.
Savannah, GA 31401
(Historic District)
Telephone: (912)236-7122
Web Site: www.17hundred90.com

Cuisine: American Regional
Executive Chef: Debbie Reid
Price Range: Lunch/$6.75~$9.25
Dinner/$16.50~$25.95

Veal Medallions with Lemon Caper Butter

8 veal medallions, cut ¾ inches
   thick from center loin
1 to 2 tablespoons of olive oil
Seasoned flour
¼ cup white wine (not a sweet wine)
½ lemon (or more, if preferred), juiced

1 small can artichoke
   hearts, drained
1~2 tablespoons of capers
Salt and pepper, to taste
1 stick unsalted butter,
   cut into small pieces

Cover veal with plastic wrap and pound, with a meat mallet, to less than ¼ inch thick. Preheat oven to 180 degrees. Heat a sauté pan and add olive oil after pan is hot, but not smoking. Dredge veal lightly in flour, shaking off excess. Add medallions to sauté pan in batches, being careful not to crowd the pan. Cook until golden brown on both sides, about 1 to 2 minutes on each side. Add more olive oil, as needed. When done, place meat on an oven-proof platter and keep warm. After all medallions are cooked, deglaze pan with wine and lemon juice; cook until reduced. Add remaining ingredients. Whisk butter into sauce and continue whisking until butter is incorporated and sauce is creamy. Spoon sauce over veal medallions and serve.

Yield: 4 servings

Roasted Rack of Lamb

| 2 rack of lamb | Salt and pepper, to taste | 1 teaspoon olive oil |

Preheat oven to 425 degrees. Salt and pepper racks and set aside. Add oil to skillet and add lamb when oil is hot. Sear meat-side down about 2 minutes. Turn over and cook same amount of time on other side. When lamb is well-seared, take out and let cool. Pour off excess oil and deglaze pan for sauce. Set aside.

Mustard Coating

3 tablespoons of Dijon mustard
 (use ½ grain and ½ regular
 Dijon mustard)
1-2 cloves fresh garlic, chopped

2 teaspoons fresh rosemary
1 teaspoon Lawry's seasoning salt
¼ teaspoon freshly ground pepper

Combine all ingredients. Using a pastry brush, apply coating over entire surface of meat (except the bones).

Bread Crumbs

½ cup Progresso seasoned bread crumbs
½ teaspoon garlic powder

½ dry mustard

Roll coated meat into seasoned bread crumbs. Pan spray an oven-proof pan and put meat in pan, rack side down. While meat is cooking, finish preparing sauce (below). Using a meat thermometer, cook meat to desired temperature or until center is 130 degrees (about 15 to 20 minutes). Take out of oven and let sit for 5 minutes. Cut between the bones and divide meat into 4 servings.

Sauce

| 1 cup beef stock | Kitchen Bouquet |

Add beef stock to frying pan, where deglazing has been done, and season to taste. Add a little Kitchen Bouquet to darken, if desired. Serve over sliced lamb.

Yield: 4 servings

17 Hundred 90 has been a gourmet tradition in Savannah for over a century and has been acclaimed as "the most elegant restaurant in Savannah" by *Gourmet Magazine*

A recent edition of *Georgia Trend* magazine singled out 17 Hundred 90 as a favorite spot for "financiers, business people, and professionals."

The Boar's Head

Casual Fine dining, in an old cotton warehouse, overlooking the Savannah River

Address: 1 North Lincoln Street
Savannah, GA 31401
(Waterfront)
Telephone: (912)651-9660
Web Site: http://savannahmenu.com/
boarshead

Cuisine: New American Cuisine
with a Southern Flair
Executive Chef: Philip Branan
Price Range: Lunch/$8-$15
Dinner/$15-$25

Philip Branan's Black-Eyed Pea Soup

¾ pounds dried black-eyed peas
¼ pound bacon, diced
1 cup white onion, chopped
1 cup celery, chopped
1 cup carrot, chopped
2 cloves garlic, minced
¾ cups diced tomatoes, with juice
1 cups fresh collards, rinsed,
stems removed, diced

1½ quarts rich chicken stock
½ smoked ham hock
½ teaspoon kosher salt
¼ teaspoon dried oregano
⅛ teaspoon dried thyme
⅛ teaspoon ground white pepper
⅛ pound cooked ham, diced
½ tablespoon chopped fresh cilantro
1 ounce sherry

Soak peas overnight in cold water. Render bacon in a large, heavy-bottom soup pot over medium heat. Add next 3 ingredients and cover. Cook until onions are soft, about 10 minutes. Add garlic and cook about 10 seconds. Drain peas and add to the pot, along with tomato and collards. Cover with stock and add the ham hock. Season with next 4 ingredients. Bring to a boil. Reduce heat to low and simmer, covered, for about 1½ hours. Remove ham hock and dice any meat left on bone. Return hock to pot, along with diced ham and cilantro. Finish with sherry and adjust seasonings, if necessary.

Yield: ½ gallon

Boar's Head Grill and Tavern Savannah Trifle

Vanilla Custard Sauce

1 cup sugar	8 egg yolks
1 quart heavy cream	1 tablespoon vanilla
Dash of salt	1 tablespoon Grand Marnier

Put first 3 ingredients in a heavy-bottom pot. Scald. Place yolks in a stainless steel bowl and whip until lemon-colored. Once cream is scalded, slowly pour half of cream into yolks, whipping slowly. Next, temper yolk mixture back into remaining cream--slowly whipping, all the while. This tempering process prevents the yolks from scrambling. Put mixture back on low heat; cook, stirring with a wooden spoon, until custard sticks to back of spoon. Remove from heat and add last 2 ingredients. Cool completely before putting away.

Assembly

1 sponge cake (made or purchased)	Whipped cream
1½ ounces of Grande Marnier	Sliced almonds, toasted

Ladle 1½ cups sauce into bottom of 8-inch crystal bowl. Top with a layer of cake. Sprinkle Grand Marnier on top of cake. Repeat process for other two layers. Top third layer with Grand Marnier, custard, whipped cream, and toasted almonds. Fruit may be added for a festive touch.

Yield: 8-10 servings

In *Romantic Days and Nights in Savannah (2001)*, Georgia Byrd cites The Boar's Head as Savannah's "Most Romantic Restaurant"

"Great black-eyed pea and ham soup-- everything is made from scratch, the old-fashioned way!"
--*Savannah Magazine*, June 1999

The first restaurant on Savannah's famous River Street

Bodi's Sophisticated Palate and Homemade Desserts

A delightful find on Savannah's Southside

Address: 238 Eisenhower Drive
Savannah, GA 31406
Telephone: (912)355-6160
Web Site: www.eatinginsavannah.com/
bodis.html
Cuisine: All types

Proprietor: Richard Halperin
Price Range: Breakfast/$3.95-$7.95
Lunch/$5.95-$8.95
Note: Also sells specialty gourmet
food products and cooking aids.

Curried Chicken Salad with Mango and Cashews

3 pounds chicken breasts, poached
(discard skin and bones; cut meat
into bite-size pieces--about 4 cups)
2 tablespoons fresh lemon juice
2 mangoes, peeled, pitted, and
cut into ¾ inch pieces
1 cup chopped celery
4 scallions, including green part, minced

¼ cup plain yogurt
¼ cup mayonnaise
1½ teaspoons curry powder
½ teaspoon ground cumin
1 cup roasted cashew nuts, chopped
2 tablespoons chopped
fresh coriander, if desired
Salad greens

In a large bowl, toss together first 3 ingredients. Add next 2 ingredients. In a small bowl, whisk together next 4 ingredients. Add dressing to chicken mixture with salt and pepper to taste. Combine the salad together well. Just before serving, stir in cashews and coriander. Serve the salad, at room temperature or chilled, arranged atop salad greens.

Yield: 6 servings

Contributor's note: *Grapes and walnuts may be substituted for mangoes and cashews.*

Richard's Oatmeal Cookies

1½ cups sifted flour
1 teaspoon salt
1 teaspoon baking soda
1 cup butter
1 cup packed brown sugar
1 cup sugar

2 eggs
1 teaspoon vanilla extract
3 cups rolled oats
1 cup chopped pecans
1 cup raisins

Sift together the first 3 ingredients. Cream butter and sugars in a mixing bowl until light and fluffy. Beat in eggs. Add sifted dry ingredients and mix well; stir in vanilla. Blend in remaining ingredients. Drop by teaspoonfuls onto greased cookie sheets and bake at 350 degrees for 10 to 15 minutes, or until lightly browned.

Yield: 3 dozen medium-sized cookies

Two-Version Praline Cheesecake
Graham Cracker Crust

1 cup graham cracker crumbs
¼ cup finely chopped pecans

¼ cup butter, melted

Combine all ingredients in a bowl and mix well. Press over the bottom of a 9-inch springform pan. Chill.

Filling

24 ounces cream cheese, softened
1¼ cups packed brown sugar
3 eggs

2 teaspoons vanilla extract
1 cup whipping cream

Beat cream cheese in a mixing bowl until light and fluffy. Gradually beat in 1 cup of sugar. Beat in the eggs 1 at a time, mixing well after each addition. Stir in remaining ingredients and pour into prepared crust. Sprinkle top with remaining ¼ cup brown sugar. Bake at 450 degrees for 10 minutes and then reduce temperature to 275 degrees. Bake 1 hour. Cool on a wire rack. Remove side of the pan and place onto a serving plate.

Yield: 6-8 servings

Featured in the *Savannah Morning News*
May 30, 1999

Johnny Harris Restaurant

Serving the "Best Barbeque" since 1924

Address: 1651 E. Victory Drive
Savannah, GA 31404
Telephone: (912)354-7810
Web Site: www.johnnyharris.com

Cuisine: American
Price Range: $4.95-$18.95
NOTE: *Johnny Harris BBQ sauce may be
ordered online or by calling 1-888-547-2823

Grilled Pork Steaks

½ (12-ounce) can beer
2 tablespoons of margarine
3 bay leaves
Salt and white pepper, to taste

Ground garlic
4 pork steaks
1 cup Johnny Harris BBQ sauce*

Pour beer into a sauce pan; add margarine and seasonings. Allow mixture to simmer. Trim away all but a small amount of fat from the edges of meat and score edges in several places (prevents meat from curling). Grill steaks for 15 to 20 minutes over medium-high heat, turning frequently. Brush on sauce after each turn and, again, on both sides immediately before removing from grill.

Yield: 4 servings

Editors' Note: *Try serving with a baked Vidalia onion--cored, stuffed with butter and a beef bouillon cube, and baked at 350 degrees (or microwaved) until tender.*

Steak Au Poivre

½ cup black peppercorns
5 tablespoons olive oil
2 tablespoons, plus 1 teaspoon butter
4 (¼-inch thick) strip steaks,
  thinly cut

¼ cup minced shallots
¼ cup cognac or brandy
½ cup rich beef stock
4 tablespoons chopped tarragon
Salt and pepper, to taste

Crack peppercorns by crushing them against a cutting board with side of a heavy knife or bottom of a pan. Press peppercorns into sides of steaks. Heat oil with 2 tablespoons of butter in a heavy skillet. Cook steaks, turning occasionally, until cooked to desired doneness. Remove steaks from pan and keep warm while preparing sauce. Add shallots to pan and sauté until translucent. For next step, be careful as cognac creates a large flame. Add cognac or brandy to skillet and light with a match. Shake pan above burner until flame dies out. Add beef stock and cook over high heat. Whisk in remaining butter and tarragon. Season to taste with salt and pepper. Serve sauce over steaks.

Yield: 4 servings

BBQ Shrimp Stir-Fry

½ pound shrimp, peeled and cooked
1 cup broccoli florets
1 cup cauliflower florets
1 cup sliced carrots

1 cup cherry tomatoes
1 cup sliced mushrooms
1 cup Johnny Harris BBQ sauce*

Combine all the ingredients in a wok, pour barbecue sauce over top, and stir until vegetables are tender and cooked through. Excellent served with rice.

Yield: 1 serving

Johnny Harris BBQ sauce chosen "favorite sauce"
in nationwide contest. -- *Bon Appetit* (1996)

"To enter the door at Johnny Harris Restaurant
is to step back to a time when eating out was a special treat."
--Richard Allen, *Savannah Morning News* (1997)

Out of 31 sauces, Johnny Harris' BBQ sauce was voted number one
in its category. -- *Food and Wine* (1989)

The Lady and Sons

Good home cooking in an atmosphere of true Southern hospitality

Address: 311 W. Congress Street
Savannah, GA 31401
(Historic District)
Telephone: (912)233-2600
Web Site: www.ladyandsons.com
Cuisine: Southern

Proprietor: Paula H. Deen
Price Range: Lunch/$5.99-$14.99
Dinner/$14.99-$21.99
Cookbook: *The Lady & Sons*
Savannah Country Cookbook,
Published by Random House, Inc.

Bubba's Beer Biscuits

4 cups Bisquick
¼-½ cup sugar

1 (12-ounce) can beer
2 tablespoons butter, melted

Preheat oven to 400 degrees. Mix ingredients well, adjusting the sugar according to how sweet a biscuit you prefer. Pour into well-greased muffin tins. Bake for 15 to 20 minutes. Serve with honey butter (see page 24).

Yield: 2 dozen biscuits

Squash Casserole

2 cups cooked, mashed yellow squash
2 cups Ritz cracker crumbs
1 cup evaporated milk
1 cup shredded cheese,
such as Cheddar or Swiss
1 cup onion, chopped

2 eggs, lightly beaten
1 teaspoon salt
1 teaspoon pepper
Pinch of sugar
6 tablespoons butter

Place squash in a large bowl. Add next 4 ingredients and stir well. Stir in remaining ingredients and pour into a greased 1-quart casserole. Bake at 350 degrees for 40 minutes.

❧❧❧❧❧❧❧❧❧❧❧❧❧❧❧❧❧❧❧❧❧❧❧❧

Baked Spaghetti

Sauce

2 cups canned diced tomatoes	¼ cup chopped fresh parsley
2 cups tomato sauce	1½ teaspoons Italian seasoning
1 cup water	1½ teaspoons The Lady's seasoned salt*
½ cup diced onions	1½ teaspoons The Lady's House seasoning**
½ cup diced green bell peppers	1½ teaspoons sugar
2 cloves garlic, chopped	2 small bay leaves

Combine all ingredients in a stockpot and bring to a boil. Reduce heat and simmer, covered, for 1 hour.

Beef and Pasta

1½ pounds ground beef	1 cup Cheddar cheese, grated
8-ounces uncooked angel hair pasta	1 cup Monterey Jack cheese, grated

Crumble ground beef in a saucepan and cook until no pink remains; drain off fat. Add the browned beef to stockpot and simmer for another 20 minutes. While sauce simmers, cook pasta according to package directions. Cover bottom of a 13 x 9 x 2-inch pan with sauce, a layer of pasta, and one-half of the cheese. Repeat layers and end with the sauce. Bake at 350 degrees for 30 minutes. Top with remaining cheese and return to oven. Continue cooking until cheese is melted and bubbly. Cut into squares before serving.

Yield: 10 servings

Editors' Note: *Lawry's seasoned salt may be substituted for *The Lady's seasoned salt. **The Lady's house seasoning may be made by stirring together 1 cup salt, ¼ cup black pepper, and ¼ cup garlic powder. Keep seasoning in a shaker.*

Ranked the "#1 International Meal in America for 1999" by Jerry Shriver, *USA Today*.

Featured on cover of *Savannah Magazine* (Sept.-Oct. 1999)

Paula Deen has appeared as a guest on

QVC	*Ready, Set, Cook*
Good Morning, America	*The Food Network*

Mrs. Wilkes' Boarding House

Address: 107 W. Jones Street
Savannah, GA 31401
(Historic District)
Telephone: (912)232-5997
Web Site: www.mrswilkes.com

Cuisine: Homestyle, Southern cooking
Executive Chef Emeritus: Mrs. Sema Wilkes
Price Range: Breakfast/$6; Lunch/$12
Cookbook: *Mrs. Wilkes'*
Boardinghouse Cook Book

Country Fried Steak

3 pounds cubed steak
Worcestershire sauce
Salt & Pepper, to taste
Pinch of garlic powder
Flour for dredging

¼ cup vegetable oil
½ cup minced onion
3¼ cups hot water
3 tablespoons flour

Place the steak in a casserole dish and generously sprinkle with Worcestershire sauce. Cover and marinate overnight. Remove from marinade and sprinkle generously with salt, pepper, and garlic powder. Dip steak in flour and shake. Heat oil and quickly fry steak until brown, but do not cook inside too much. This is done by cooking both sides on high heat, turning quickly, and then reducing heat to low to finish cooking. Boil onion in another pot with ¼ cup of water for about 5 minutes. When finished cooking as many steaks as desired, leave about 3 tablespoons browned crumbs (not burned) and drippings from steak in skillet. Add onion and 3 tablespoons flour. Stir until slightly browned. Slowly pour in the remaining 3 cups hot water as it thickens. Season with salt and pepper to taste. The gravy may be served over rice or steaks.

Yield: 10-12 servings

Editors' Note: *Always a favorite with men and good served with the vegetables on these pages.*

Fried Okra

1½ pounds fresh okra	Flour
Salt and pepper	Corn oil (or other cooking oil)

Cut the okra crosswise (not too thin) into ¾ slices. Season with salt and pepper. Toss the okra in flour and shake off the excess. Heat about ½ inch of oil in a skillet. Fry the okra over medium heat. Stir and turn until light brown and tender. Remove with a spatula and drain on paper towels.

Yield: 4 servings

Savannah Red Rice

9 medium onions, diced	1 cup tomato sauce or catsup
2 medium green peppers, diced	½ teaspoon Tabasco sauce
Bacon drippings	4 strips bacon, fried to a crisp and crumbled
2 cups cooked rice	Salt and pepper
6-8 tomatoes, chopped and cooked, or 1 (16-ounce) can tomatoes	2 tablespoons grated Parmesan cheese

Preheat oven to 325 degrees. Brown first 2 ingredients in drippings. In a large mixing bowl, combine onions and peppers with next 5 ingredients. Salt and pepper, to taste. Mix well. Pour into a greased casserole dish and sprinkle with cheese. Bake for 30 minutes or until rice is dry enough to separate.

Yield: 4-6 servings

Editors' Note: *The addition of 1 pound of cooked shrimp, ground beef, sausage, or ham will transform this Lowcountry classic into a delicious one-dish meal.*

"At age ninety-four she (Mrs. Wilkes) is the queen of all she surveys, the grande doyenne of Southern dining." -- John T. Edge, 2000

Winner of the 2000 James Beard
America's Regional Classics Restaurant Award

Featured in *The Atlanta Journal, The Belgian Weekly Gazette, Bon Appetit, Esquire, The Boston Globe, The New York Times, Pittsburg Post-Gazette, Redbook, Savannah Morning News, Sky, Southern Living, Time, Town and Country,* and profiled on David Brinkley's evening news program.

Soho South Cafe

Where food is an art

Address: 12 W. Liberty Street
Savannah, GA 31401
Telephone: (912)233-1633
Web Site: www.sohosouthcafe.com

Cuisine: American Comfort
and European Flair
Chef: Bonnie Retsas
Price Range: $6.95-$9.75

Crab and Asparagus Quiche

1 (10 inch deep-dish) pie shell
3 whole eggs
2 egg yolks
1 cup heavy cream
1 cup sour cream
1½ cups Gruyère cheese
1 whole shallot, minced,
    then sautéed in 1 teaspoon
    butter until soft; cooled
¼ cup Boursin cheese
1 tablespoon minced dill

1 tablespoon minced tarragon
1 teaspoon salt
¼ teaspoon white pepper
⅛ teaspoon cayenne
¼ teaspoon nutmeg
1 bunch fresh asparagus, trimmed
    and blanched for 3 minutes in
    boiling, salted water; cooled and
    sliced crosswise
½ pound jumbo lump crabmeat,
    picked over

Line pie shell (and up the sides) with single piece of parchment paper. Fill with dried beans, rice or pie weights. Bake in 350 degree oven about 10 minutes or until crust is pale golden brown. Whisk together first 16 ingredients. Mix in asparagus and crab. Bake at 325 degrees for 1 to 1¼ hours, or until filling is set and no longer jiggles.

Yield: Serves 6-8

Editors' Note: *Good served with sliced cantaloupe or other fresh fruit.*

᭞᭞᭞᭞᭞᭞᭞᭞᭞᭞᭞᭞᭞᭞᭞᭞᭞᭞᭞᭞᭞᭞᭞᭞

Mixed Berry Shortcakes

Shortcakes

3 cups all-purpose flour

1 whole egg

1 rounded tablespoon baking powder

1 egg yolk

½ teaspoon salt

2 cups heavy cream

½ cup sugar, rounded

1 teaspoon vanilla

8 tablespoons butter, cubed

1 tablespoon orange zest (rind)

Stir dry ingredients together in a large bowl. Cut butter into dry ingredients. Whisk remaining ingredients together in a smaller bowl. Mix egg mixture into dry ingredients using a rubber spatula (hold some of the liquid back in case you don't need it all). Dough should be moist. Turn dough out onto floured surface; pat into 1-inch thick circle. Cut into 8-9 rounds and place on a parchment-lined baking pan. Place in freezer for 15 minutes. Brush tops lightly with cream and sprinkle tops with sugar. Bake in 400 degree oven for approximately 17 to 20 minutes or until a sharp knife inserted in center comes out dry.

Berries

3 quarts of mixed berries
(strawberries, blueberries, raspberries, and blackberries)
1 cup sugar
Juice of an orange

Slice strawberries and mix with remaining berries. Add sugar and juice of an orange. Let macerate for at least one hour or until sugar dissolves and juices are released from berries.

Whipped Cream

1 quart heavy cream   ½ cup powdered sugar   1 teaspoon vanilla

Beat together in cold bowl, with a cold whisk, until cream holds its shape.

To serve, spoon berries onto shortcakes and top with cream.

Yield: 8-9 servings

"Dinner at Soho South is an artistic triumph"
--Richard Allen, *Savannah Morning News*

*Selected as "1 of Top 500 Restaurants" in US by
2001 Chef's Guide to American Restaurants*

Toucan Cafe

A festive atmosphere with a little Caribbean, a little Greek Isles, and a lot of whimsy

Address: 531 Stephenson Avenue
Savannah, GA 31406
Telephone: (912)352-2233
Web Site: www.toucancafe.com

Cuisine: Eclectic
Executive Chef: Jim Leclair
Price Range: Lunch/$6-$10
Dinner/$10-$20

Eggplant Torte

1 medium to large eggplant
1 tablespoon salt
½ cup flour
Pinch thyme, basil, salt, and pepper
2 eggs
Cooking oil

8 ounces spinach, wilted
¼ cup creamy feta
1 tomato, sliced
Tomato basil sauce (any type)
Sliced provolone cheese
1 cup roasted orzo pasta

Peel and slice eggplant. Season with salt and let stand for 10 minutes; pat dry. Add seasonings to flour. Dip eggplant into flour and then into egg. Cook in lightly oiled pan (hot, but not smoking) until eggplant is lightly browned on both sides. Top each slice with spinach, creamy feta, and a stack of 3 tomatoes. Top with tomato sauce and cheese. Cook in 400 degree oven until cheese melts and center is warm (10 to 15 minutes). Serve over roasted orzo pasta and top with tomato basil sauce.

Creamy Feta

12 ounces fresh feta cheese, crumbled
4-6 ounces heavy cream

Black pepper, to taste

In food processor, blend all ingredients until smooth.

Roasted Orzo Pasta

Place dried orzo in 400 degree oven 8 to 10 minutes until browned. Cook in boiling salted water until tender. Strain and serve with eggplant.

❧❧❧❧❧❧❧❧❧❧❧❧❧❧❧❧❧❧❧❧❧❧❧❧❧

Tilapia With Smoked Corn & Crawfish Relish

Relish

2 pounds smoked* crawfish,
  veined and peeled
4 cups smoked* whole kernel corn
7 ounces hearts of palm,
  coarsely chopped
1 red peppers, finely diced
2 tablespoons cracked pepper

½ bunch green onions,
  finely chopped
3 tablespoons pesto
¼ cup red wine vinegar
⅛ cup extra virgin olive oil
Salt and pepper, to taste

Mix and chill.

Editors' Note: *A dash of liquid smoke may be used instead of a smoker.*

Red Pepper Sauce

4 roasted red peppers
1 small onion, coarsely chopped

7 green peppercorns
1½ tablespoons garlic

Mix fine in blender and add the following ingredients:

1 tablespoons basil
½ tablespoons oregano
¼ tablespoon thyme

½ tablespoons turmeric
½ cup chicken stock
Salt and pepper to taste

Heat sauce to boil.

Tilapia and Orzo

Salt and pepper
6-8 ounce tilapia filet (per serving)

Olive oil
Orzo pasta (cooked by
  package directions)

Salt and pepper tilapia. Sauté in oil

To serve, ladle Red Pepper Sauce into plate. Place a portion of orzo pasta in center of plate and top with tilapia. Garnish tilapia with crawfish relish.

Yield: 4-6 servings

Featured in *Savannah Magazine,* July-August 1999

A jewel of a restaurant, hidden off the beaten path, in the Southside of Savannah-- a must-destination!

Yanni's Greek Cuisine

A touch of the Greek Isles on Savannah's South Side

Address: 11211 Abercorn Street
Savannah, GA 31419
Telephone: (912)925-6814
Web Site: http://savannahmenu.com/
yannis

Cuisine: Greek cuisine
Proprietor: Yanni Andronikos
Price Range: Lunch/$5-$10
Dinner/$12.95-$23.95

Mousaka

3 eggplants, sliced lengthwise
3 potatoes, sliced lengthwise
Olive oil (enough for frying)
1½ pounds ground beef
1 cinnamon stick
10 whole cloves

Salt and pepper, to taste
1 onion, chopped
5 ounces whole, peeled,
and chopped tomatoes
2 tablespoons tomato paste

Fry first 2 ingredients in olive oil. Drain off oil, after frying, by placing eggplant and potato strips onto paper towels. Sauté beef in pan with seasonings, onion, and a little more olive oil. Add last 2 ingredients and cook, on low heat, until browned (about one-half hour).

Béchamel Sauce

6 tablespoons all-purpose flour
2 tablespoons butter

8 cups whole milk
Salt and pepper, to taste

Combine ingredients in a sauce pan, whisking vigorously over high heat for 5 minutes or until sauce thickens.

In a 12-inch casserole dish, layer ingredients in following order: potatoes, eggplant, beef, sauce)approximately one-half inch thick). Bake in oven at 350 degrees for 30 minutes or until sauce browns. Let stand for 10 to 15 minutes before serving.

Yield: 6 servings

ও~ও

Youlbsi
(Leg of Lamb)

Boneless leg of lamb, 4-6 pounds
10 cloves of garlic, peeled
1 cup extra virgin olive oil

3 tablespoons oregano
1 tablespoon fresh black pepper
1 tablespoon salt

Preheat oven at 325 degrees. Stuff lamb with garlic cloves. Baste outside of lamb with remaining ingredients. Cook for 2 hours. Use drippings to make a light glaze for lamb.

Yield: 18 servings

Grilled Oktapodi

1 cup extra virgin olive oil
4 tablespoons salt
Fresh octopus, 2-3 pounds

4 tablespoons oregano
Juice from 2 lemons

Oil and salt fresh octopus; hang to dry for 24 hours. Remove legs and char-grill them for 20 minutes. Baste with extra virgin olive oil, oregano and lemons.

Yield: 4 servings

Voted "Savannah's Best Southside Restaurant"
by *Creative Loafing's* Readers Poll

Beach Dreams Bed and Breakfast

Tybee Island's premiere Bed and Breakfast Inn

Address: 4 13th Street
Tybee Island, GA 31328
Reservations: 1-877-786-8866
Telephone: (912)786-9090
Web Site: www.beachdreamsbandb.com

Category: Bed and Breakfast
Owners/Innkeepers:
Ann and Keith Gay
Price Range: $90-$215

Strawberry-Orange Muffins

1½ cups strawberries, halved
3 tablespoons butter
or stick margarine, melted
2 teaspoons orange rind, grated
2 large eggs
½ cup all-purpose flour

1¼ cups sugar
1 teaspoon baking powder
½ teaspoon salt
Cooking spray
2 teaspoons sugar

Preheat oven to 400 degrees. Combine first 4 ingredients in a blender and process just until blended. Lightly spoon flour into dry measuring cups; level with a knife. Combine flour with next 3 ingredients. Add strawberry mixture to flour mixture, stirring just until moist. Spoon batter into 12 muffin cups (or 6 jumbo-sized) coated with cooking spray. Sprinkle muffins with 2 teaspoons sugar. Bake at 400 degrees for 20 minutes or until muffins spring back when touched lightly in center. Remove from pan immediately.

Yield: 12 regular-sized muffins

Editor's Note: *We also like this recipe with ½-1 cup chopped pecans added to the batter before baking.*

Crustless Quiche Florentine

½ cup butter (1 stick)
½ cup all-purpose flour
6 large eggs, beaten
1 cup milk (low-fat)
16-ounce Monterey Jack
  cheese, shredded
1 cup cottage cheese

1 cup tomato basil feta cheese
1 teaspoon baking powder
1 teaspoon sugar
1 (10-ounce) package chopped
  spinach, well-drained

Preheat oven to 350 degrees. Melt butter in a saucepan. Add flour and cook until smooth. In a large bowl, beat eggs. Add cooked mixture and remaining ingredients. Stir until well blended. Pour into a well greased 9 X 13-inch pan. Bake uncovered for 45 minutes. Cool for at least 10 minutes.

Yield: 8 servings

Breakfast Burritos

1 large tomato, diced
2 teaspoons fresh basil, finely chopped basil
(or ½ teaspoon dried basil) or salsa

In small bowl, combine the tomato and basil; set aside.

1 cup potato wedges
6 eggs, beaten
1-2 tablespoons chopped
  green chiles, optional

Salt and pepper, to taste
4 (8-inch) flour tortillas, warmed
1 cup Cheddar cheese, shredded

Spray a large non-stick skillet with cooking spray. Over medium heat, sauté potatoes until tender. Pour next 2 ingredients over potatoes; season to taste. Cook, stirring occasionally until mixture is set. Divide egg mixture evenly between tortillas, topping with cheese. Fold the tortillas over egg mixture and top with tomato/basil mixture or salsa to serve.

Yield: 4 servings.

Featured on cover of *The INNside Scoop*
(Summer 2000)

A place where life slows down enough to see it.

Georges of Tybee

Where excellence prevails in food, service, and atmosphere

Address: 105 E. Highway 80 ~~ 1 mile, on left, past Lazaretto Creek Bridge Tybee Island, GA

Telephone: (912)786-9730

Cuisine: French with Asian Influences

Executive Chef: Mir Ali

Price Range: $16-$24

Web Site: www.eatinginsavannah.com/ georgesoftybee.html

Pistaccio Encrusted Chilean Sea Bass
Festival Blend Rice

2 cups basmati rice, cooked
1 cup wild rice, cooked
½ cup toasted sliced or slivered almonds

1 cup dry cherries
2 teaspoons butter
Salt and pepper, to taste

Combine first 4 ingredients and set aside.

Pomegranate Reduction Sauce

Juice of 6-8 pomegranates   2 cups red wine   1 cup NY port wine

Slice pomegranates in half and squeeze over a strainer. Reduce all ingredients in a stainless pan or pot until syrup consistency forms. Reserve and keep warm.

Bass

Salt and pepper, to taste
6 (6-ounce) portions of Chilean sea bass
1 cup pistachios, ground up in coffee grinder

1¼ cups flour
1-2 tablespoons of olive oil
1 tablespoon butter

Salt and pepper bass. Mix pistachios with flour and encrust bass with mixture. In a medium hot pan, add oil and sear bass on each side until golden brown. Add butter and continue cooking approximately 10 minutes for each inch of thickness. In another pan, heat rice in butter, seasoned with salt and pepper, until warm. Serve bass over rice and drizzle with Pomegranate Reduction Sauce. Serve with sautéed chayote squash.

Yield: 6 servings

৯৩৯৩৯৩৯৩৯৩৯৩৯৩৯৩৯৩৯৩৯৩৯৩৯৩৯৩৯৩৯৩

Skillet Seared Yellowfin Tuna
Rice Cakes

3 jalapeños, seeded and minced
½ cup of chopped cilantro
2 eggs
1 tablespoon salt

½ cup flour
1 teaspoon baking powder
3 cups cooked Jasmine rice

Combine first 4 ingredients in a bowl. Add next 3 ingredients to make a thick paste. Fold in rice with a spatula. Form batter into one-half inch thick cakes and set aside.

Orange Sauce

3 cups orange juice (without pulp)
2 tablespoons shallots, thinly sliced
1 teaspoon hot chili paste
½ cup heavy whipping cream

1 teaspoon wasabi paste
    (more or less, to taste)
½ cup mayonnaise
1 tablespoon water

Place first 2 ingredients in a stainless steel pan or pot and reduce to 1 cup. Over medium heat, add next 2 ingredients. Reduce to 1 cup; set aside and keep warm. In another bowl, combine last 3 ingredients and set aside.

Sesame Seed Wilted Spinach and Yellowfin Tuna

Salt and pepper, to taste
6 (6-ounce) portions yellowfin tuna,
    cut into steaks
2 tablespoons olive oil

1 tablespoons butter
1 tablespoon sesame seeds
½ pound fresh spinach
¼ cup white wine

Preheat oven to 350 degrees. In a medium hot pan, sear rice cakes until crispy on both sides. Finish cooking them in oven for about 10 minutes. Meanwhile, heat a cast iron or non-stick pan on high. Salt and pepper both sides of tuna steaks and sear them in olive oil, until desired doneness (rare to medium-rare is best). In another hot pan, toast sesame seeds in butter. Add spinach and wine; cook until wilted. Season with salt and pepper. Ladle about 1½ ounces of orange sauce onto each person's plate. Place spinach on top of sauce in middle. Set the rice cake on top of spinach. Cut tuna in half and place each one on each side of rice cake.

Yield: 6 servings

Editors' Note: *These ingredients are available in most Oriental markets.*

Featured in *Southern Living* magazine (April 2000)

———————————————

"The warmly lit interior, with its appealing bar,
is perfect for a romantic evening." --*Fodor's Travel Guide* (2001)

Other Recipes

Recipes from Laurel Hill Plantation Bed & Breakfast
McClellanville, SC

Holiday Brunch Bake

1 pound bulk breakfast sausage
1 (4-ounce) jar chopped pimento, drained
1 (10-ounce) box frozen chopped spinach,
    defrosted and drained
1 cup all-purpose flour
¼ cup Parmesan cheese

1 tablespoon instant minced onion
1½ teaspoons Italian seasoning
½ teaspoon seasoning salt
8 eggs
1 cups milk
1 cup shredded Cheddar
    or provolone cheese

Cook sausage and drain. Sprinkle cooked sausage on bottom of greased 9 x 13- inch baking pan. Top with ½ jar pimento and spinach. In small bowl, combine next 5 ingredients. In large bowl, beat eggs and milk. Add flour mixture to egg mixture and beat well. Pour beaten mixture over spinach. Bake in preheated 425 degree oven for 20 to 25 minutes or until set. Top with remaining pimento and cheese. Bake 2 to 3 more minutes or until cheese melts. Cut into squares.

Yield: 10 servings

Apple Egg Casserole

4 eggs, beaten
1½ cups milk
1 tablespoon sugar
1½ cups biscuit mix
1 (21-ounce) can apple pie filling
½ teaspoon cinnamon

⅛ teaspoon nutmeg
2 cups shredded sharp cheese
½ stick butter, melted
1 pound ground sausage,
    cooked and drained (optional)

Beat eggs and add next 2 ingredients, blending until smooth. Mix apples with spices and spread in a 13x9x2-inch baking dish. Sprinkle cheese over apples and cover with batter. Pour melted butter over batter and bake at 350 degrees 50 to 60 minutes or until golden brown. Serve warm.

Yield: 4-6 servings

Hash Brown and Sausage Casserole

2 pounds sausage (hot or mild)
2½ cups shredded Cheddar cheese
1 can (10 ¾-ounce) can
  cream of mushroom soup
1 cup sour cream
1 (8-ounce) container of French Onion Dip

1 cup chopped onion
¼ cup (each) green and red bell
  pepper, chopped
Salt and pepper, to taste
1 (30-ounce) package frozen hash
  brown shredded potatoes, thawed

In a skillet, cook sausage until browned. Drain well. In a large mixing bowl, combine the next 7 ingredients, seasoning with salt and pepper. Fold in thawed hash brown potatoes. Mix well. Spread ½ of the hash brown mixture over bottom of a 9x13-inch greased baking dish. Spread ½ of browned sausage over hash browns. Repeat layering with second ½ of hash brown mixture. Top casserole with remaining sausage. Bake at 350 degrees for about one hour or until casserole is golden brown.

Yield: 10 servings

Baked Tomato Halves

4 large tomatoes
8 tablespoons butter or margarine,
  divided
½ cup finely chopped onion
2 teaspoons prepared mustard

1 teaspoon Worcestershire sauce
4 slices white bread,
  torn into coarse crumbs
4 teaspoons chopped parsley

Preheat oven to 350 degrees. Wash tomatoes and remove stems; cut in half crosswise. Place tomatoes, cut side up, in shallow baking pan. In 4 tablespoons of hot butter in skillet, sauté onion until tender. Stir in mustard and Worcestershire. Spread onion mixture on tomatoes. Melt remaining butter in skillet; add bread crumbs and parsley. Sprinkle crumb mixture over tomatoes. Bake, uncovered, 20 minutes or until heated through and crumbs are golden brown.

Yield: 4 servings

To order a copy of Jackie Morrison's cookbook featuring her private collection of Laurel Hill Plantation recipes, send a check or money order for $8.50 (tax and postage included) and the address where the cookbook should be mailed:

Jackie Morrison
Laurel Hill Plantation
P. O. Box 190
McClellanville, SC 29458

NOTE: *Jackie and Lee Morrison hosted a never-to-be-forgotten bed and breakfast inn (see page 8) for 14 years where memorable breakfasts were consistently served. Jackie, who served as president of the South Carolina Bed and Breakfast Association before retiring from innkeeping in 2001, compiled this cookbook at the insistence of her well-fed guests.*

Maxine Pinson's
Potpourri of Ice-cream Recipes

Basic Vanilla Ice-Cream

2 (14-ounce) cans sweetened condensed milk
1 quart half-and-half

1 tablespoon, plus 1 teaspoon,
   vanilla extract

Combine all ingredients, mixing well. Pour ice-cream mixture into freezer can of a 1 gallon hand-turned or electric freezer. Freeze according to manufacturer's instructions.

Yield: 2½ quarts

Note to WeightWatchers' Point Counters: When fat-free sweetened condensed milk and half-and-half are used, a heaping cup of the Basic Vanilla Ice-Cream is only 2 points!

Variations

Coffee Ice-Cream: Combine ¾ cup hot water and 1 tablespoon instant coffee granules, stirring until granules dissolve. Let cool slightly. Stir coffee mixture into ice-cream mixture just before freezing.

Mocha Ice-Cream: Combine 1 cup hot water and 1 tablespoon instant coffee granules, stirring until granules dissolve. Let mixture cool slightly. Stir coffee mixture and 1 (5.5-ounce) can chocolate syrup (½ cup) into ice-cream mixture just before freezing.

Toffee Ice-Cream: Stir 1 (6-ounce) package toffee-flavored candy pieces into ice-cream mixture just before freezing.

Mint Chocolate Chip Ice-Cream: Stir ½ cup green crème de menthe and 1 (6-ounce) package semi-sweet chocolate mini-morsels (1 cup) into ice-cream before freezing.

Butter Pecan Ice-Cream: Add 1 tablespoon butter flavoring and 2 cups coarsely chopped toasted pecans to ice-cream mixture just before freezing.

Lemonade Ice-Cream: Add 1 (6-ounce) can frozen lemonade concentrate, thawed and undiluted, to ice-cream mixture before freezing.

Cherry-Pecan Ice-Cream: Substitute 1 teaspoon almond extract for vanilla, and add ⅓ cup maraschino cherry juice to ice-cream mixture; freeze ice-cream as directed. Stir ¾ cup quartered maraschino cherries and ¾ cup chopped pecans into ice-cream after freezing.

Strawberry-Banana-Nut Ice-Cream: Stir 3 bananas, mashed; 1 pint strawberries, coarsely chopped; and ¾ cup chopped pecans into ice-cream mixture just before freezing.

Peanut Butter Ice-Cream: Stir ¾ cup chunky peanut butter into ice-cream mixture just before freezing. Serve ice-cream with chocolate syrup, if desired.

Double-Chocolate Ice-Cream: Stir 1 (5.5 ounce) can chocolate syrup (½ cup) and 1 (6-ounce) package semi-sweet chocolate mini-morsels (1 cup) into ice-cream mixture just before freezing.

Black Forest Ice-Cream: Stir 1 (5.5-ounce) can chocolate syrup (½ cup) and 1(16 ½-ounce) can pitted Bing Cherries, drained and halved, into ice-cream mixture just before freezing.

Chocolate-Covered Peanut Ice-Cream: Stir 1 (5.5-ounce) can chocolate syrup (½ cup) and 2 (7-ounce) packages chocolate covered peanuts (2 cups) into ice-cream mixture just before freezing.

Cookies and Cream Ice-Cream: Break 15 cream-filled chocolate sandwich cookies into small pieces: stir into ice-cream mixture just before freezing.

Editors' Note: *Fat-free condensed milk and fat-free half-and-half are now available at most grocery stores.*

"Our Foods staff has taken the liberty of naming Maxine Pinson of Savannah the queen of ice-cream. We first planned to test her basic recipe and six variations. But we enjoyed all those so much that we picked three more flavors to test--then chose six more. We think you'll get carried away with this recipe, too."
-- *Southern Living*
(August 1988)

Just relaxing--a delightful B&B indulgence

"INNformation for INNgoers"

Q & A Section for Inngoers

Topics

All of the answers refer specifically to smaller bed and breakfasts (approximately 2-8 rooms/suites) or historic inns (approximately 9-25 rooms/suites). For easier reading, the term "inn" is used in reference to each, with clarifications made as needed. The questions are topically arranged, and the responses are divided into 2-4 parts (*only selected ones include quotes from innkeepers and "inn tales from inn trails"):

- **Brief response to question**

- **An "expanded" answer**

- ***Quotes from innkeepers in direct response to question**

- ***An "inn tale from the inn trail" relating to the issue**

The "INNformation for Inngoers" section of *Lowcountry Delights* is being developed into a book, *INNside Scoop* (see page 168) and enlivened with lots of "inn tales from inn trails." Authored by Maxine Pinson, it is being published by The B&B and Country Inn Marketplace and scheduled to be available by the end of 2002.

Note: *The B&B's and historic inns shown in this section have each been reviewed or recommended in The INNside Scoop B&B newsletter during the past few years. Each is one of The INNside Scoop's top rated inns, based upon discerning criteria, and represents a sampling of the types of inns available. The photographs are randomly placed and do not, necessarily, relate to the juxtaposed questions being addressed. More information on these inns, including reviews on many, may be found at:*

www.innsidescoop.com
The Web sites of these inns are listed on page 159

How I Got Hooked on B & B's

Bill in front of Mrs. Hudspith's B & B in Edinburgh, Scotland
The old photograph is faded, but the memories remain vivid.

I experienced my first B & B (bed and breakfast inn) during a trip to Ireland in 1971. My husband, Bill, and I were only there one night, but that was all it took for me to become a B & B aficionado forever. Now, over thirty years later, my enthusiasm for B & B's continues.

During the summer of 1971, while Bill was an exchange student at Exeter University Law School in England, we had opportunities to visit Ireland, France, Italy, Scotland, Spain, Germany, Belgium, Holland, and Switzerland. Relying upon *Europe on Five Dollars A Day,* a travel guide published by Arther Frommer for budget-conscious travelers, I developed our itinerary and made reservations at B & B's in each country.

Of all the B & B's we experienced, our most memorable was a small B & B in Edinburgh, Scotland. It was located on the street where *The Prime of Miss Jean Brodie,* by Muriel Spark, was filmed. Each morning, from our seat at the breakfast table, we watched a horse-drawn milk wagon making deliveries to homes along the cobble-stoned street in suburban Edinburgh.

The innkeeper, Mrs. Hudspith, was a wonderful Scottish lady who kept a fire blazing in the dining room and a table covered with freshly baked goodies. A pot of tea, warmed by a knitted teapot "cozy," stayed full. If it had not been for her kitchen guard dog, Bruce, I would have been tempted to sneak into her kitchen, after hours, for more of her homemade treats. Perhaps, that is why big-eyed Bruce was stationed in that particular spot--and he *never* left. I tried being nice to the mongrel, but he just glared and growled at me. I soon realized there was no use in trying to make a truce with Bruce. I thought it really annoying that this inhospitable Scot had to share the same name of my favorite cousin and our Scottish forebear, king Robert the Bruce.

It was sitting around Mrs. Hudspith's communal table, next to a warming fire after a day of touring in drizzly weather, that I became forever enamored with B & B's. I love meeting new people and sharing stories. There is no better place for doing this than B & B's.

How could I ever forget Mr. and Mrs. Willy from Vancouver, an octogenarian couple we met over breakfast at Mrs. Hudspith's? We stayed in touch for years. When our first child was born, Mrs. Willy crocheted a little pink cap and sent it to her. Each Christmas Bill and I received alluring Canadian calendars from the Willys, always accompanied by an invitation to visit them. I hoped we might be able to one day, but we never were. Our chance meeting was a "one moment in time" experience through which I feel my life was enriched.

Since that memorable trip in 1971, I have stayed at a variety of highly acclaimed resorts and world-class hotels, within the States and abroad. However, none of my fancy hotel experiences—from The Waldorf-Astoria in New York City to Rome's Grand Hotel Plaza--have provided me with the same cherished memories as those I have from favorite B & B's. There is a major difference between simply *staying* somewhere and *experiencing* a place in its totality. I prefer the experiential, and I doubt my love for the wonderful world of B & B's will wane.

Definitions and Distinctions

ॐॐॐॐॐॐॐॐॐॐॐॐॐॐॐॐॐॐॐॐॐॐॐॐॐ

> *The following definitions attempt to codify what is presently being used in the field. They are only approximations and will vary by region or individual innkeeper.*
>
> ---
>
> Reprinted, with permission, from PAII
> (The Professional Association of Innkeepers International)
> www.paii.org

Homestay, Host-Home

This type of establishment is an owner-occupied private home where the business of paying guests is secondary to its use as a private residence. The hosts are primarily interested in meeting new people and making some additional monies while continuing their present employment or retirement. Frequently located in residential areas, zoning or other government restrictions may prevent the use of signs, public advertising, etc. Usually between 1-3 rooms, these homes are often a member of, and usually inspected by a reservation service organization (RSO) but are rarely required to be licensed or inspected by local applicable governmental agencies. Breakfast is the only meal served. In some instances, it may be an unhosted apartment where breakfast is self-serve.

Bed and Breakfast

Formerly a single family dwelling usually in the 4-5-room range, this owner-occupied establishment has an equally mixed use as home and lodging with lodging superseding home more often than not. It is located in a legally zoned area and meets all the tax, fire, building and health requirements for this size and use of property. This establishment advertises publicly and can legally post a sign. Like the homestay or host home, because of its size, these B&Bs usually cannot support a family unit, so the B&B is often one partner's job and the other has outside income.Often the property is purchased specifically to be a B&B, but many are converted family homes. Reservations may be made directly with the property.

Bed and Breakfast Inn

Generally small, owner-operated businesses providing the primary financial support of the owner. Usually the owner lives on premises. The building's primary usage is for business. Inns advertise, have business licenses, produce their own brochures, comply with government ordinances, pay all appropriate taxes and post signs. Breakfast is the only meal served and only to overnight guests. The inn may host events such as weddings, small business meetings, etc. Room numbers range from 4-20 with a small, but increasing number up to 30. Reservations may be made directly with the property. Note: The distinction between a "B&B" and a "B&B inn" is not readily apparent, except with regard to building usage.

Country Inn

A business offering overnight lodging and meals where the owner is actively involved in daily operations, often living on site. These establishments are, in fact, B&B inns which serve at least one meal in addition to breakfast, and operate as "restaurants" as well as overnight lodging accommodations. Modified American plan (MAP) country inns serve dinner to overnight guests only, and the cost of dinner and breakfast is generally included in the room rate. A country inn with a full-service restaurant serves these additional meals to the general public. To be a country inn, a property does not have to be located in a rural area. Room numbers tend to range from 6 to 30. To understand bed-and-breakfast/country inn in the context of other properties that are confused with bed and breakfast, the following definitions are included:

Bed & Breakfast / Self-Contained Cottage

A detached building affording privacy and seclusion to guests, with owner providing minimal services. Breakfast is either delivered to the room, taken with others in a central dining room or placed prior to arrival (or upon daily cleaning) in the cottage kitchen facilities. Owner is usually available for questions, but generally guests choose this style of B&B when they want little help. Certain geographic regions see this type of lodging more than others. The light personal touch and memorable B&B decor further distinguish this genre from the vacation rental/condo.

Bed & Breakfast Hotel

These are 30+-room historic properties offering breakfast that can only be considered hotels. Only the historic structure, and perhaps some decorating components and breakfast provide the B&B feel.

Summary

Although all of the above categories view themselves as providing these below-listed characteristics, in reality, the larger the property--and particularly if the owner is not actively involved in daily operations and guest interaction--the property moves rapidly into the "hotel" perception in the minds of the traveller.

- Generous hospitality and personal attention to guests
- Architecturally interesting or historic structure
- Owner involvement in business
- Clean and comfortable ambiance and surroundings
- Individually decorated rooms

Burke Manor Inn
Gibsonville, NC

Basic Differences Between Inns
and Traditional Accommodations

Q: What are advantages of staying at an inn?

A: The defining uniqueness is found in the distinctive characteristics each individual inn promises to provide. Inns are as different and individualistic as the innkeepers who run them, and they lack the sterility often associated with more traditional types of lodging. Personal service and guest pampering are trademarks of the inn industry. A stay at a bed and breakfast or historic inn is likely to be far more memorable than staying at a motel or hotel (many which now attach "inn" to their name).

Many inns are located within historic dwellings and provide an opportunity for personally experiencing fascinating homes in a way many would be unable to do otherwise. For individuals who are "people people," an inn provides an ideal setting for meeting and interacting with interesting people from all areas of our country and abroad. For those desiring privacy in their own zone, there are inns that are totally secluded. See "Why I'm Hooked on B&B's" (p. 130).

One innkeeper presents a challenge to travelers: "Try going back to an inn for a second time and compare your treatment to what you receive when returning to a chain hotel." Another innkeeper relates, "I have started having more guests coming just to get gardening and/or decorating ideas. I know one caterer who frequents inns for recipe collecting."

Q: What are differences distinguishing the inn experience from a traditional stay at a chain hotel or motel, especially one which refers to itself as an "inn" and includes breakfast with the room?

A: The human factor and personal touches. Attention-to-detail. Having an opportunity to meet and interact with other guests. Memorable, home-cooked breakfasts—not pick-up items from the neighborhood donut shop or styrofoam coffee cups with stick stirrers.

Most inngoers can tell you the names of the innkeepers at their favorite inns long after their visit at the inn. Many times, they can name new friends or acquaintances met while there. I challenge anyone to tell you the name of a desk clerk at some non-descript motel or the name of a tuxedoed concierge at a swanky resort once the visit ends. How often have you met new friends or fascinating conversationalists while staying at a motel or hotel? As far as distinguishing between breakfasts at a traditional chain hotel/motel and the morning repast at an inn—well, there simply isn't a comparison. Breakfasts at inns vary as much as the inns serving them. The meal may be simple, plentiful, or a grand 3-course feast.

Q: Aren't inns primarily for the wealthy or socially elite?

A: Absolutely not. There is a bed and breakfast or an inn to suit every taste, budget, and personality. When you are ready to travel, spend some time checking out different inns on the Internet until you find one that appeals to you. Four good Web sites to begin with are:

www.innsidescoop.com
(less expansive than the others, but it includes a listing of outstanding inns in 30 states)
BedandBreakfast.com
TravelGuides.com
www.innmarketing.com/bbguide.htm
(lists numerous B&B links)

Victoria House Bed & Breakfast
Hampton, VA

Q: Are inns more or less expensive than traditional motels/hotels?

A: Many people think inns are cost-prohibitive. Not true. It is true that inns, especially larger historic inns, can be quite pricey. Inns located in popular tourist areas will always be more expensive than ones located in smaller towns or areas with fewer attractions, but some of these off-the-beaten-path inns are true gems. If you compare the price paid with the benefits received, you will discover inns are more affordable than you might suspect. Inns range from rural to urban, historic to modern, elegant to practical.

Expensive inns often offer special packages and a wide range of rooms at varying prices. Some offer special rates to civil servants. Even the big chains, including ones promising to "leave the light on for you," aren't that cheap anymore. I consider the majority of inns fairly priced, considering their offerings and services. I feel some inns are worth more than they charge, while some are over-priced. If cost is a concern, clarify the details of what you will be receiving when you make your reservations.

Melange Bed & Breakfast Inn and Gardens
Hendersonville, NC

Q: Are there additional charges I might incur when staying at an inn?

A: My biggest pet peeve is when there is an unposted local charge for telephone calls made. Local calls, made from an inn, are usually free. Be aware of a possible parking expense if you are staying in a district where parking spaces are at a premium; you may need to purchase a city parking permit (around $6 for 2 days in Savannah). Some inns provide them; others do not. Most inns do not charge for wine served at their wine reception or snacks/beverages in a guest refrigerator. Some do. If the inn has a staff, tipping is appreciated. Sometimes a service charge, for the room, is built into the rate. Just ask the innkeeper, when the reservations are made, about any questions you may have.

Q: Are walk-ins accepted at inns like at traditional motels/hotels? Sometimes, when traveling, I like to remain flexible and plan my trip as I go.

A: Typically, hotels and motels have a staff member on duty round-the-clock. Most inns do not. Rooms are limited at inns and sometimes reserved far in advance. However, if a "walk-in" arrives during an inn's standard check-in time (usually between 3-7 p.m.) when there is availability, most innkeepers will accept the guest without a reservation.

Finding availability at an inn is much less likely on week-end nights or during a high-season period. Of course, cancellations can always occur at the last minute any day of the week or time of year. It is not advisable to start looking for an inn when you are tired of driving and ready to stop for the night. There are no billboards, along expressways, telling you where the next inn is located. Even if there were, just popping-in and finding a room available is less likely than at chain-type lodgings.

Not all innkeepers are keen on accepting guests without a reservation. One innkeeper explains why: "Some inns promote having fresh flowers and/or fruit in a guest room upon the arrival of a guest. This is not always possible with a walk-in or a last minute reservation." Once again, it depends upon the policy of the inn and the innkeeper.

Q: Are most inns open year-round like traditional accommodations?

A: Yes. However, some inns close during seasons when few visitors come to their area, such as during the months of bitter cold in certain parts of New England. This information is usually posted on an inn's Web site. Larger inns (especially ones with a staff) are usually open year-round. Smaller ones usually close on Christmas Day so the innkeepers can spend time with their family. Sometimes a small inn closes for a month in January (or several weeks at another time during the year) so the innkeepers can have a break or make repairs (usually done in January). It varies with the inn.

Q: What type of work do innkeepers do for a real job when they aren't taking care of guests?

A: Permit me to enlighten you, my friend. Innkeeping *is* a real job! Innkeepers are some of the hardest working people I know and their down-time is rare. Innkeeping is a job a lot of wanna-be's romanticize, but they are clueless about the degree of work it entails. I am sometimes asked if I would ever consider opening a bed and breakfast. My answer is a two word exclamation: "No way!"

Q: What did the majority of innkeepers do in "their other life?"

A: There is no stereotypical innkeeper any more than there is a stereotypical guest. They come from all walks of life, and their backgrounds run the gamut from A - Z.

Q: How about inngoers. Is there a profile for them?

A: They, too, come from all walks of life.

One innkeeper says, "Generally speaking, B&B's attract guests who are more educated and sophisticated than average. Guests often find breakfast to be an interesting and entertaining experience."

The Importance of an Inn's Affiliation
with a Professional Organization

Q: How important are ratings (such as AAA and Mobil) of inns?

A: With so many inns from which to choose, ratings help narrow the focus by letting one know the quality or service they may expect from a specific inn.

I have personally discovered unrated inns which I consider superior to some of the inns I have visited with a high rating from a prestigious organization. Even though Mobil and AAA are usually reliable in their ratings, just because an inn chooses not to be rated—for whatever reason—is not a reason to avoid going to it. Sometimes an excellent inn has not been in business long enough to undergo the inspection required for a rating.

A: A long-time innkeeper, of a successful and established inn, raises an important point. "It is important to remember that the ultimate test of an inn's quality is experiential. Owners of older establishments, under the same ownership for several generations, may not feel compelled to pay the fees of joining certain groups, even though they may meet or exceed the criteria of the various standards of the inspection." Another experienced innkeeper states, "Many of their requirements are not necessary. In some cases, they can actually detract from an inn's uniqueness."

Q: How important is an inn's affiliation with a professional inn group, and what are some of these established organizations an inngoer should know about?

A: Very important. Affiliation with established associations provides assurance to the inngoer that certain basics (such as cleanliness, food codes, and safety) have been met and approved. But, keep in mind, the quality of an inn is not a prerequisite for becoming a member of state bed and breakfast associations, PAII (Professional Association of Innkeepers International), or similar type organizations.

Most state associations set standards that must be met, including periodic inspections. Inclusion in a bed and breakfast directory (online or in most travel guides, unless stated otherwise) requires nothing more than payment for inclusion. Some private groups are more exclusive than others and issue invitations (with a hefty fee) for membership.

Amenities and Attention-to-Detail

Q: What types of amenities may I expect at an inn?

A: The extent of amenities varies with the inn and may be restricted to the basics or exceed the bounds of one's imagination. Amenities at an inn may include: clock radios, televisions/VCR's, CD players (sometimes with CD's), terry cloth robes (sometimes slippers), an array of toiletries (shampoo, conditioner, body lotion, make-up remover cloths, etc.), hairdryers, an iron and ironing board, working fireplace, whirlpool tub, European showers, heated bathroom floors, heated towel racks. The list continues ad infinitum.

One creative innkeeper tucks fresh lilac into a roll of lavendar-colored netting, tied on the ends with lavendar satin ribbon, between the pillows at turn-down. She sprays the bed linens, when ironing them, with a lavendar spritz made with vodka.

Safety Issues

Q: Is it safe for a woman, traveling alone, to stay at an inn?

A:. Very. It is probably the safest place a woman traveling alone can stay.

As a travel writer, I often travel alone when reviewing inns. I have never experienced an inn where I felt safety was an issue of concern.

Q. Do I need to lock my bedroom door when staying at an inn?

A: Yes. I have been to a few inns, but only a few, that do not have a lock on the bedroom door. Small towns, as a whole, are more lax with door locking than urban areas. Larger inns sometimes provide a small safe in guest rooms or in the inn's office for the safekeeping of valuables when the guest is away from the inn.

Personally, I am not interested in hearing about the theft-free history of an inn or how well-to-do the guests in residence may be. When I leave costly computer and camera equipment in my room, I want the security of knowing that door is locked. Insisting upon a locked room is not an unreasonable request, even if the most valuable thing in there is your favorite pair of sneakers.

Bonnie Castle
Grantville, GA

Children and Pets

Q: Do innkeepers ever have children living at home?

A: Yes, but it is the exception. If the innkeepers have older children living at home, they sometimes assist their parents, in different capacities, with the innkeeping.

Q: Are inns appropriate for children?

A. Most are not, even though they may be accepted at a certain age. Children are much happier at a family-oriented type of lodging. Inns do not cater to children, and sometimes their behavior causes discontent with other guests.

A gourmet breakfast, along with interaction with other adult guests, can be ruined by a crying baby or an ill-mannered child. Many couples go to an inn to get a reprieve from children.

One innkeeper says, "I don't think a couple on honeymoon would appreciate toddlers running around on hardwood floors above their honeymoon suite. Older children often find breakfast conversation, an integral part of the B&B experience, to be boring."

Q: Do B&B's object to guests bringing pets to stay in their room with them?

A: Most inns do not permit pets. Those that do usually have a notice posted on their Web site. Some inns offer barns for equestrian travelers who travel with their horse(s) in tow. As always, whenever in question, just ask. But, do not expect all inns to accept furry friends.

There are cat-lovers inns where cats are assigned to each guest and share their room. I know of inns which have bended their rules, under extenuating circumstances, so a guest could bring along their dog, bird, or guinea pig. Many innkeepers have pets of their own, and some are very territorial. There are inns, though rare, which offer a special "silver service" treatment for pets. One inn offers services complete with silver bowls and bottled water set upon an Italian linen napkin! The only restriction is that the pet must be caged (in the room) when the owner is not around.

Business Travel and Special Needs

The Duke Mansion
Charlotte, NC

Q: Do inns cater to business travelers?

A: Most definitely. Some have mini-suites, complete with a kitchen, for regulars who stay a week or more at a time (usually at a lower rate). Inns catering to business travelers customarily offer fax and copier services, private telephone lines, and an early breakfast option. Some even have a mini-office set up for business guests.

Most innkeepers do not object to faxes being sent to their guests within reason. Sending lengthy documents is not acceptable. One innkeeper tells the story of a thousand page deposition faxed to an attorney staying at their inn. Not to be done!

Q: Are most inns set up for guests who are physically challenged in some way?

A: More and more inns are offering special accommodations, always at ground level, for physically challenged guests. If there is a possibility you might encounter a problem at the inn, because of a physical situation, be sure to discuss it with the innkeeper when you call to inquire or make a reservation. They will be able to provide the assurance you need or help you find another place better suited for your particular needs.

Inn tale: When it is time to shower, make sure you are not wider than the stall. One inn guest got stuck in a shower stall in Georgia and couldn't get out. He was traveling with a friend, who had a room across the hall. When his friend heard the yelp for help, he performed a successful rescue operation--with the help of a bar of slippery soap and some hefty tugging.

Selecting an Inn

Q: How do I know what an innkeeper considers "nice" is the same thing I consider nice?

A: You don't. Asking an innkeeper if their inn is "nice" is kind of like someone asking if you think your own child is "cute." Of course, an innkeeper thinks their inn is nice. And, even if is not quite up to the standards they wish it were, I do not think an innkeeper is likely to say, "Well, not really..."

We each have our own mental image of what adjectives depict. What I may consider nice, cozy, elegant, luxurious, or gourmet may not be in sync with an innkeeper's concept of these words at all. Even guests will differ on the accuracy of adjectives applied to an inn. Concepts are formed by one's personal frame-of-reference and life experience--it does not mean one is right and the other is wrong.

Q: I have found that inns do not always measure up to the glorious images portrayed in their brochures or Web sites. How can I know whether what I see online is what I'll find on-site?

A: Not finding on-site what is promoted online (or in a slick, glitzy brochure) is my greatest pet-peeve of the industry. Of course, this is not something limited to B&B's or inns. I prefer selecting an inn whose Web site or brochure shows as many photographs as possible (guest rooms, dining area, common areas, outside areas). I also like to have an idea of the neighborhood. Virtual tours are excellent as they provides 360 degree coverage of the rooms and surrounding area outside. If an inn's Web site offers one, take advantage of it.

If an area is blatantly absent, my radar starts beeping. For example, if there are beautiful photographs of the common areas, but none of the guest quarters--or vice versa. Of course, there are all sort of techniques for improving the appearance of a photograph. Pay attention to the furnishings and decor, if that is something important to you. Also, I find innkeepers who take care to provide a high-quality, informative Web site usually run a high-quality inn. Be wary of inns using superlatives and claims with nothing to back them up.

Inn tale: I will never forget the time I went to an inn proclaiming (online and in the state B&B directory) that they had the *best* breakfast in the state. Says who? Apparently, the innkeeper had not visited some of the stellar inns, with gourmet fare, in that state that I have had the opportunity of experiencing. The same inn had a sign, in front of their inn, stating their yard was the "yard of the month"--in small letters, beneath this announcement, it stated: "proclaimed by the owner." I find such claims misleading and deceptive, not cute or amusing.

Getting the Best Rates

Q: Do inns offer seasonal rates?

A: This is usually dependent upon the location of the inn and the degree of tourism in the area at specific times of the year.

It is almost impossible to get a room (unless reserved a year in advance or more) in Savannah for the green week of Savannah's annual St. Patrick's Day festivities. However, incredibly low rates (in comparison to the usual rates) are often offered at different Savannah inns during the slower months of January and February. Look on the Web sites of inns for specials offered, or call and inquire if seasonal rates are not noted on the inn's Web site.

Q: Can I get a room for less if I am not interested in breakfast or clean-up service?

I have only been to a few inns willing to reduce the rate if you are not interested in the daily clean-up service. This option is primarily restricted to long-termers. Of course, you may always ask—but please respect the policy the innkeepers have decided upon, whatever it may be.

Harmony House Bed & Breakfast
Rock Hill, SC

Contacting an Inn

Q: Why is a toll-free and a regular telephone number often listed for an inn?

A: A toll-free number is established specifically for making inquiries, reservations, or cancellations. Most innkeepers do not object to calls being made on their toll-free line to let them know you are arriving later or earlier than originally scheduled.

It is not acceptable to leave an inn's toll-free number with your children, a baby-sitter, or anyone else for the purpose of contacting you during your stay at the inn. Neither is it acceptable for a personal message or greeting to be delivered to you via an inn's toll-free line.

One innkeeper reveals, "Some inns have an 800 number monitored through another organization who forwards the call to the inn. So, there may be times when the toll-free call you are placing will not go directly to the inn you are calling."

Q: When is the best time to call an inn?

A. The best time to call smaller inns is between 10 a.m.–5 p.m. local time (never during the time breakfast is being prepared/served or late at night). Larger inns, with a staff on duty, may receive calls until 10 p.m.--especially in vacation cities.

Restrain from becoming annoyed if an answering machine picks up instead of a real, live person—especially if the inn is small and does not have someone to mind the phone round-the-clock. For most innkeepers of small inns, a wireless phone is like an extra appendage. But they cannot be available to answer the phone at all times. They do have shopping to do and personal business to tend. When calling an inn outside your locale, be aware of the time zone.

If a potential guest from the East Coast calls an inn on the West Coast at 8 a.m., the phone will be ringing out there before the rooster crows. See if you can find the information you need on the inn's Web site. Almost all inns have one now. Actually, if I can't see an inn online, I seldom consider it--which is why I feel so strongly about online honesty in true representation of an inn.

Making, Securing, and Canceling Reservations

Q: Do most inns offer online availability and online reservations for guests?

A: More inns are offering online availability and online reservations. Some inns provide an online room chart indicating which rooms are available on which dates. This service provides a valuable convenience for both inngoer and innkeeper, in addition to minimizing telephone calls and costs. Online availability shows which rooms are available, at that moment, so online reservations may be made and secured.

A disadvantage of online reservations is that it eliminates valuable discourse between an innkeeper and a potential guest. Engaging in a one-on-one conversation, with an innkeeper, allows the inngoer to get a feel for an innkeeper's manner and style. This is important since an inn is, in essence, a reflection of the innkeeper who manages it. Smaller B&B's are likely to require a phone call follow-up so the innkeeper can also get a feel for the type of inn the guest is seeking. This way, the guest is more likely to get the property best suited for specific desires and needs.

An innkeeper says, "We update our online availability manually, and so it may not always be current. If *no availability* shows, it is best to call the inn just to double-check for accuracy."

Q: Do inns require reservations to be guaranteed?

A: The majority of inns do require reservations to be secured by a credit card and usually have their policy stated on its Web site or brochure.

Many inns require an advance deposit. Be sure to find out if they are just holding your credit card number or actually charging your card. Smaller B&B's (and even some medium-sized historic inns) are not set up to accept credit cards and require payment with cash or check. The standard requirement is full payment for one night; however, it may be more for extended stays, during a "high season," and times of special events.

Q: What if I need to cancel my reservations?

A: If the need for cancellation arises, call the innkeeper as soon as possible. Most innkeepers are willing to accommodate whenever they can, but revenue from the renting of rooms is what keeps them in business. Cancellation policies vary, but most inns have theirs posted on their Web site and must adhere to them. Sometimes an inn will provide you a gift certificate (usually valid for one year) to use when you can come.

Smaller inns often fill up far in advance during special seasons or local events. When there is a last-minute cancellation, the room is more difficult to fill since many would not expect the inn to have an opening. Above all, respect the inn's cancellation policy, and most innkeepers will work with you in working out arrangements mutually satisfactory.

Q: Are inns willing to rent out their entire facility to a group?

A: Most inns (small B&B's as well as larger ones) often rent out their entire facility to wedding parties or private groups.

Because of the home-like atmosphere of B&B's, they provide an attractive option for a variety of private functions

Angel Arbor Bed and Breakfast Inn
Houston, TX

Almost All Inns Have Private Baths

Q: I stayed in B&B's in Europe, and I often had to share a bath with other guests. I do not like sharing a bath with strangers, and so I do not go to inns anymore.

A: Almost all American inns have private baths for *each* of their guest rooms--and I would say 98% of them are adjacent to the bedroom. If a bath is shared, it is usually located between two rooms rented by guests traveling together. An inn's Web site and brochure indicate whether its accommodations include a private bath or not.

Occasionally, a room has a private bath, but it is located across the hall. When this is the case, a robe is usually provided for the guest, and a sign is posted that the bath is a private one (reserved for guests staying in a particular room). In older structures, finding a way to provide an adjacent bath, for each guest room, often provides a challenge--one which sometimes escapes a satisfactory solution.

Packing for an Inn Stay

Q: Is there any set dress code for guests staying at inns?

A: No. Most guests (and innkeepers) dress according to the "2C" code: casual and comfortable, even at the more formal inns. If you see someone dressed up, they are probably a business traveler, on the way to an appointment, or someone going to a dress-up affair.

If the inn has a swimming pool or a hot tub, they probably provide terry cloth robes (usually mentioned on the Web site). But, just in case they do not, take a cover-up along. The common areas of an inn are no place to strut your stuff--not even if it the inn is beachside.

Q: Even though I am an adult, I still have a favorite pillow and stuffed animal I like to sleep with. What will an innkeeper think when my sleeping companion is found snuggled on my special pillow?

A: Believe me, innkeepers have seen it all! I have also learned a lot of people have a "special" pillow they prefer sleeping on and often carry it with them when they travel.

Hawkesdene House
Andrews, NC

Arrival, Check-out, Settling up

Q: Is there a procedure I should follow if I need to arrive before or after regular check-in times?

A: This is an easy question to answer. You simply do the same as you would want an expected personal guest to do if visiting in your home. *You call* and let the innkeeper know when you will be arriving, and you call again if that changes. To do otherwise is rude. Read my lips on this one: *to arrive early or late, without calling, is rude, rude, rude.*

When you call to let the innkeeper know you are running late (or to ask if you may arrive earlier than originally scheduled), a courteous and sincere "I hope this will not be an inconvenience to you" is always appreciated. I don't know about you, but I really get annoyed when someone doesn't show up, within a reasonable time frame, when they tell me they will be arriving. Innkeepers are no different. The innkeepers of smaller inns often have no out-side help, and it is thoughtless to keep a busy innkeeper waiting for hours on end for a late arrival. Sometimes they arrange their schedules specifically for the arrival of a guests. It is equally ill-mannered to arrive hours in advance of the agreed-upon time of arrival. Most innkeepers, I know, are caring individuals who worry when guests have not shown up or called hours after they are expected. I hear more complaints about early and late arrivals, from innkeepers, than all others combined. The bottom line: don't do it—not even to "just drop your bags off and use the bathroom."

Q: When I arrive at an inn, do I ring the doorbell or just walk on in?

A: Depends on the inn's size and location. B&B's usually keep their entrance door locked. There may be a note indicating whether you should knock, ring the bell, or go to another entrance. Larger inns, with a staff member seated within viewing distance of the door, often have the door unlocked so guests may let themselves in.

Some inns have a telephone on the porch so the innkeeper may be called when you arrive. One of my favorite inns has an ornamental iron gate at the estate's entrance. Guests are given the code before arrival. After keying it in, the gate swings open--to paradise!

Q: If I am interested in staying at an inn, but do not have reservations, may I just let myself in for a peek-about?

A: No siree--never! Remember, B&B's are also private homes. Would you want someone to just walk into your home for a little "peek-about"?

Inn tale: One innkeeper retired from innkeeping after a father and his child walked in on her taking a bath in the private quarters of her B&B.

Q: If I see an inn I would like to stay at, but no one is there to check me in, may I just select a room and check myself in?

A: If I had not heard a story of someone who actually did this, I would consider the question too preposterous to dignify with a response--which, of course, is *no*.

Inn tale: An innkeeper, a lady who has a secluded mountain inn and never locks the en-trance doors during the day, returned home to find a guest who had taken the liberty of checking himself in. Walking in, with a bag full of groceries, she was greeted by a man wearing an inn robe and sipping a glass of sherry.

Q: Will I have to listen to the history of an inn, or go on a grand tour of rooms and grounds, before being shown to my quarters?

A. "Orientation time" varies from inn-to-inn, and it is a requirement of some organizations to which inns may belong. However, most innkeepers realize that guests—especially those who have travelled a long distance—are anxious to be shown their room and get situated. Often an innkeeper will ask if you'd like to see the inn "now" or "later." Usually, "later" is the wiser answer. On warm or cool days, an innkeeper may offer you something hot or cold to drink upon your arrival. And, for heaven's sake, if you need to use the restroom upon arriving, ask where it is! You can be polite and attentive to inn stuff afterwards. First things first!

Q: What if I do not like my accommodations when I get to the inn?

A: Most innkeepers are not happy if their guests are not happy. If you are displeased with your room, ask the innkeeper if there is another room available that you may have instead. Be prepared to pay more if it is an upgrade. If a legitimate problem develops in your room (plumbing, heating, etc.) that is beyond your control and which cannot be corrected within a timely period, you are entitled to another room, if available, at no extra charge.

Q: If I feel I have legitimate complaints about the inn or the innkeepers, is there someone I can register my concerns with?

A: Check the inn's Web site or brochure to see if the inn is affiliated with a state organization or PAII. If so, contact one of these groups about the problem. If you would like to address the innkeepers directly, refrain from addressing your grievance in front of other guests.

Q: When do I pay for my room at an inn?

A: This varies with the personal preference of the innkeeper. Some innkeepers prefer getting "the unpleasantries" over and done with at the beginning; others prefer waiting until check-out time, especially if they anticipate additional charges being added to your account.

Inn on Covered Bridge Green
Arlington, VT

Gratuities and Additional Charges

Q: Are there any other charges I might incur while staying at an inn?

A: Not usually. If there are, it is usually at the larger inns. If you feel there might be, just ask when you make reservations if there are additional costs involved (such as a service charge). If parking is a problem in the area of the inn, you may be required to purchase a parking permit in order to park on the street. Some inns provide these for their guests at no charge.

But the parking permit is usually far less than the charge would be for parking in a hotel garage.

If you need to make local calls or need to go online, check to see if local calls are free. Typically, there is an information book in each guest room at an inn with basic information. If there is a charge, it will probably be noted in this book. I have never stayed at a B&B where there is a charge for local calls. However, sometimes larger inns charge up to 75 cents per local call. This is not customary at an inn presenting itself as a B&B--a fact I always make a point to bring to the management's attention.

Q: Is there a standard tipping policy at inns?

A. Just as each B&B is different, so is the question of tipping. Whether you stay in a B&B, inn, motel, or hotel, it is courtesy to leave $1 to $5 per night for the housekeepers; I usually leave the money on the dresser. The exact amount varies with the length of the stay, the price of the property, the size of the room, and the services rendered. If the B&B is quite small, and the owners do the housekeeping themselves, no tip is necessary. Since many people are unaware of this practice, many innkeepers have taken to leaving tipping envelopes as a gentle reminder to guests, although there is no obligation to leave anything, especially if the housekeeping is not up to par. Personally, we don't much care for the practice, and would prefer a no-tipping policy, with the housekeepers paid a good wage, but recognize that that's not always possible. If you're not sure, it's always okay to ask. Last but not least, remember that inns which include accommodations, breakfast, and dinner in the rates typically add a 15% service fee to the entire amount. (*Reprinted by permission of Sandra W. Soule, Editor, BedandBreakfast.com*)

Breakfast Time at Inns

Q: When staying at a B & B, am I expected to eat at the same table and socialize with other guests?

A: Some inns have individual tables where a single traveler or a couple may eat alone. This is especially true at the larger historic inns. But, at a typical B&B, expect to share breakfast at a table of strangers who, chances are, will become friends before the meal is over.

No innkeeper (I hope!) is going to make you talk to anyone else or start the day off with any of those aggravating little "ice-breaker, talk-maker" games. But, if you are at a communal table, having breakfasts with other guests, it is customary and polite to at least say "howdy." Newspapers are not read at the table to the exclusion of other guests. As a rule, I have found guests at inns to be friendly folk whose company I thoroughly enjoy.

Q: What kind of food is served for breakfast at inns? Is the menu comparable throughout the week, or does it vary on the week-ends?

A: Everything imaginable: simple, Continental, deluxe, a full country breakfast, a gourmet breakfast, a 3-course feast (which usually begins with a fruit dish, followed by a breakfast entrée, and finished off with something sweet). Most inns begin breakfast with a fruit course. For guests who desire coffee upon rising, it is often available in a special area—sometimes with a basket of muffins. Some inns will deliver a coffee tray to your room, upon request.

Typically, breakfast at a B&B or an historic inn is more than a meal. It is an event. I have been introduced to foods at the breakfast tables of inns that I have not been familiar with previously. Larger inns sometimes offer a menu, but this is unusual. A few inns provide a menu selection, the night before, from which breakfast selections may be made. Most innkeepers will ask, sometimes when the reservations are made, about food allergies or restrictions (dietary, religious, or other). Some innkeepers post the breakfast menu in a creative manner.

Q: What time is breakfast served?

A. It varies with the inn. Some innkeepers just have one seating, but most offer a time span (i.e., 8 a.m. - 9:30 a.m).

Most innkeepers are willing to accommodate their guests however they can. If a guest has an early flight or an early business meeting, an early breakfast can often be arranged.

Inn at Wintersun
Fairview, NC

Q: When traveling, I enjoy meeting important people who are intelligent and in my socio-economic class. I don't hobnob or eat with just anyone. Will I be able to meet people like me at inns?

A. I sincerely hope not—and I particularly hope I never end up across the table from you. If you are primarily interested in picking up new names to drop (or impressing others with your importance), it would behoove you to seek your ilk elsewhere.

Even though inngoers include celebrities and high-profile individuals, around the breakfast table everyone is just "Jane" or "Joe."

Q: I am accustomed to saying a blessing at breakfast. Are blessings said at the breakfast table of most inns?

A. A blessing is not customarily said at an inn's communal breakfast table. However, saying grace is an individual choice. A guest may bow his head and bless his food, without a comment to anyone but the one to whom thanks are being offered.

Q: When eating at a communal table, must I wait until everyone is seated before I may begin eating?

A. Absolutely not. Breakfast, at an inn, is not like a seated dinner or a formal banquet. For the most part, the modus operandi at inns is very laid-back and amazingly casual—much more than most people realize or anticipate.

Q. Do innkeepers usually join their guests at breakfast time.

A: Some do, but most do not.

Q: If I finish eating, before the other guests, may I excuse myself and leave the table.

A: Certainly.

Q: When I first get up in the morning, I don't like to talk. When I am traveling alone, I prefer eating alone. Will an innkeeper feel obligated to sit and "keep me company," during breakfast, if I am the only guest at the inn?

A: This might happen occasionally, but not usually. For one thing, innkeepers have a full agenda in the morning. Sometimes an innkeeper will ask if you would like for them to sit with you. If you prefer eating alone, just say so in a courteous manner.

Q: Is it necessary to get dressed for breakfast at an inn?

A: Even though you may feel quite at home at an inn, especially a smaller B&B, it is not appropriate to show up for breakfast in your nightie, robe, stocking feet, or barefoot. Even though bare feet are not acceptable, bare heads (no baseball caps or curlers, please) are preferred. Other than that, as long as you are dressed decently, almost anything goes. There is no right or wrong dress code at inns, and most people dress casually. I do not see a problem sauntering down, for a cup of early morning coffee, in a cover-all robe.

One innkeeper says, "the tone of an inn sets the stage for appropriate dress."

At the Inn Alone

Q: If I am at an inn alone and the phone rings, should I answer it?

A: Not unless the innkeeper has requested that you do so.

Q: If I am at the inn alone and someone comes to the door, should I let them in?

A: Unless it is another guest, who you know is staying at the inn, you should *not* let anyone in.

Q: If I am alone at an inn before going to bed, should I turn off all the lights?

A: No. Some inns have their lights on timers. Smaller inns usually have a procedure for turning off lites before retiring. For insurance and safety purposes, certain lights are left on so guests can go and come comfortably.

Q: I love exploring new places—opening closed doors and looking into the cubby holes. Is this okay to do while staying at an inn?

A: If there are closed doors, with or without privacy signs, do *not* open them. They are closed for a reason.

Q: Should I call the innkeeper by his or her first name?

A: That is the preference of most innkeepers, and they will probably call you by your first name (unless you indicate otherwise).

Schell Haus
Pickens, SC

Q: Do innkeepers ever keep any of their clothing or personal belongings in the closets or drawers of the guest quarters?

A: Only rarely--and it is something the industry considers inappropriate.

Q: If I need something from the kitchen when the innkeeper is not around, is it permissible to go in and get it?

A: No, not unless the innkeeper has, specifically, invited you to do so. Some state health department regulations forbid guests from entering an inn's kitchen. If you see a "private" sign on the kitchen door, interpret it as a polite way of saying: "Stay out."

Q: Is it acceptable to ask an innkeeper to use their car if I have flown in and do not wish to rent one.

A: No, it is *not* acceptable.

Q: If I am flying in, is it appropriate to ask the innkeeper to pick me up from the airport?

A: Not unless they promote a pick-up service, which only a few do. Otherwise, rent a car or hail a taxi.

Q: Is it acceptable to ask an innkeeper to do my personal laundry or to request permission to use the inn's laundry facilities?

A: I suspect most innkeepers would be thrilled to do your laundry *if* you would not mind taking some of theirs home to do in return. But, unless you are willing to do that, then you need to do your *own* laundry (or pay to have it done by someone who is in the laundering business—innkeepers are not). Neither is it appropriate to ask for permission to use an inn's laundry facilities. However, if you are a long-termer at the inn, the innkeeper may offer the use of the laundry facilities to you. If so, provide your own supplies.

There is a distinct difference between service and servitude. An innkeeper's charge is to provide the former, not the latter.

Q: I love candles and incense and often travel with my own. Is it acceptable to burn candles at an inn?

A: Always ask for permission before burning candles. Incense is best left at home. It travels through an inn's heating/air-conditioning system, and its aroma is not appreciated by everyone. Open flames often violate an inn's insurance coverage.

Be aware that "blackening" the wicks of candles is the proper way of displaying them. It does not provide license for burning the candles.

Inn at Celebrity Dairy
Siler City, NC

Q. What if I have an accident while at a B & B (soiled sheets, become ill, etc.)?

A. Even though accidents are embarrassing, the innkeeper (or housekeeper, if there is one) needs to be notified as soon as possible. Accidents happen, and it is better for the innkeeper to hear about it from you—especially if it involves breakage or a stain that needs immediate attention to keep from becoming permanent. If the damage is significant, then offering to pay for its repair or replacement is the least you can do.

Telephone and Internet Access

Q: *My work requires that I travel with a laptop and have online access. Is this available at most inns?*

A: The majority of inns now have a telephone in each guest room, and the larger ones often have private guest lines (sometimes with an answering machine or voice mail). More and more inns are now providing modems for laptop computers in guest rooms.

Smaller inns are less likely to have telephones in guest rooms. Those that do not have phones in guest rooms usually have a guest phone (set up in a private area) or a cordless phone that can be taken into one's room. If there is a telephone in your room, make sure that using it for Internet access will not interfere with business calls to the inn or disable other guests from using the phone. When a telephone line is shared by guests, an innkeeper will sometimes post "Internet guidelines" for usage. You will also need to check to see if a "9" needs to be dialed in order to get an outside line.

Q: *Should I give the inn's main telephone number as a number where I can be reached while staying there?*

A: Calling a guest on a business line should be reserved, primarily, for emergency calls. If you anticipate receiving calls during a visit at an inn and do not have a cell phone of your own, ask the innkeeper (before arriving) how you may be contacted. If you will have a private line in your room, the innkeeper can give the number to you in advance.

The Use of Alcohol and Illegal Drugs While at an Inn

Q: *Is taking a cooler, filled with iced-down beer, to an inn acceptable?*

A: Save the beer-filled coolers for a tail-gate event or for week-ends at Motel 6. Walking through a family-run B&B or an elegant historic inn, carrying a cooler, is tacky. If you are staying in a stand-alone cottage, on the premises of an inn, then it is okay.

What might not be acceptable in one situation might be perfectly acceptable in another.

One innkeeper says: "I've never objected to coolers in my guest rooms. However, guests are usually considerate enough to ask first. We cater to nature-based tourism, and our guests often need coolers for their excursions." Another says, it doesn't bother us since a lot of guests don't want to go out to dinner, but I wouldn't show up carrying a cooler instead of a suitcase."

Q: *Is there a policy concerning the use of alcoholic beverages at inns?*

A: The use of alcoholic beverages varies with the inn and the legalities of the area where the inn is located. Many inns offer wine (at an afternoon wine reception) and/or cordials at turn-down. However, the availability of hard liquor at inns is not customary. Again, this question/answer section is referring, specifically, to smaller B&B's or historic inns, not country inns.

Q: I don't care about little afternoon teas or wine receptions. When 5 o'clock comes, I want a real drink. Will I be able to get the ice and set-up I need at an inn?

A: Listen up, sweetheart. If you want a real drink, then be real sure you can handle it without becoming loud or offensive to other guests. This applies, of course, to any drinking. Innkeepers are happy to provide ice and often have ice-buckets available that you may take to your room. Loud and rowdy partying, at an inn, is not tolerated. An inn is not a tavern.

Q: Can I smoke pot, in my room, while at a remote little B&B way off the beaten path?

A: The use of illegal drugs is never acceptable at an inn, no matter how remote it might be. Don't even think about it.

Inn Tale: One guest decided to give it a try, but it didn't work. The innkeeper was also a county police officer and picked up the odor right away.

Et Cetera

Q: Is it okay to use bubble bath in an inn's whirlpool tubs?

A: It depends on the individual model. Whirlpool tubs vary in operation and range of capability. Instructions are often posted in the bathroom. If you have any questions about its use, check with the innkeeper prior to using it.

Q: What if you can't figure out how to operate the tub? Some are so fancy and high-tech!

A: Same answer as above.

Inn Tale: The only time I have ever had to call an innkeeper, after hours, was when I could not figure out how to turn off an ultra-modern soaking tub. It required more computer knowledge, to operate its digital keypad, than I have--and I work with computers all the time.

Q: What if there are bugs in my room?

A: All inns use a pest control service, but some of these rascals are impossible to get rid of entirely--like the infamous Palmetto water bug (euphemism for roach) that likes to creep around the Lowcountry. Ladybugs love B&B's and seem to converge upon them.

One innkeeper framed a poem she wrote about how much ladybugs adore her inn.

Inn note: At one of the most elegant inns I have experienced, a roach jumped onto my pillow just as I was getting ready to lie down upon it. Another time, I found a dead "water bug" floating in a top-rated inn's toilet--one that even had the "seal-of-cleanliness" paper strap across it. *Bugs happen.*

Q: I enjoy picking up memorabilia from inns I visit. Do inns ever offer, for sale, special items reminiscent of their inn?

A: Definitely. Small corner or "cupboard" gift shops are frequently found in inns, and they often offer a wide variety of items with the inn's name or logo. Items include mugs, terry cloth robes, artwork, cookbooks, Christmas ornaments, magnets, and a host of other things to remind you of your stay at the inn.

My home study is dotted with mementos from visits to inns and special mementos given to me by innkeeper friends.

Inn at Warner Hall
Gloucester, VA

Q: Is it okay to take food into my room at an inn?

A. Avoid taking in "fast food" or pizza into inn rooms. Doing so can result in stains, an offensive lingering smell (which can float into other rooms), and result in problems with rodents and/or ants. However, if a snack is provided at the inn, innkeepers usually do not object to you carrying it to your room. Just make sure not to put wet-bottomed glasses onto stainable wooden furniture or marble tops. Always use coasters, when provided.

Q: Is it okay to take some of the inn's hangers with me if I need extra ones?

A: No problem. Just mail them back when you get home--just in case the next guest needs an extra one. It shouldn't be any more trouble for you to mail hangers back to the inn than for the innkeeper to go purchase replacements for the ones you take.

Q: Are the toiletries sitting out for me to keep?

A: The individual (not the pint-sized) containers are provided for your convenience, and you may certainly take whatever you do not use with you. But, please, leave the extra rolls of toilet paper and tissue at the inn. You only pay for your needs while at the inn.

If staying at an inn straps you financially to the point that you will not be able to afford to purchase your next roll of toilet paper, then, perhaps, you should consider more budget-oriented accommodations.. Inns are not paper product providers. Rule of thumb: never tuck anything into your suitcase or garment bag that you would be embarrassed for the innkeeper to discover if an "inspection check" were being made. Most guests are totally trustworthy.

Q: What should I do if I leave something at the inn? Will the innkeeper be willing to mail it to me?

A: Most inns have a "lost and found" box. Just call and let the innkeeper know what you left and the area (if you know). Chances are, you are more likely to have it returned than if you had left it at a motel or hotel. However, it is the responsibility of the guest to pay for the postage and handling of a returned item.

If you should inadvertently take the inn's keys home with you, the innkeepers would appreciate your thoughtfulness in mailing them back to the inn as soon as possible.

Q: Is it okay to make suggestions, face-to-face to an innkeeper, on how I feel their inn could be improved?

A: Most innkeepers are appreciative of helpful suggestions. Just remember, an innkeeper's inn is their "baby," and sometimes suggestions are not wanted or appreciated.

Unless I am specifically asked for recommendations by an innkeeper, I usually do not offer them. When grievances are voiced, always express them to the innkeeper privately. PAII (Professional Association Innkeepers International) often reminds innkeepers: "A complaint is a compliment," which is also the title of a book addressing this issue.

Q: Are the guest books found in the bedrooms of many B & B's for compliments, suggestions, or both?

A: Most innkeepers hope guests will record something positive about their visit in the guestbook. Suggestion cards are often left out for appraisals and comments.

These books are not intended for writing odes of love to your beloved or anything of an offensive nature to others.

Q: Is it okay to take home a book from an inn's library that I have not completed reading or a video that I would like to view?

A: Even with the best of intentions, things "promised to be returned" often are not. Some inns offer a "book swap" program so guests may take a book in exchange for leaving one behind. However, it is best not to put an innkeeper on the spot by asking for the special favor of taking home a book or video. Magazines found in guest rooms, except for the local freebies, are to be left in the room for future guests.

Q: When I would like to express gratitude, in a special way, to an innkeeper for extra kindnesses extended me during my visit, how can I do this?

A: Just a hand-written thank-you note, expressing your gratitude, is always appreciated and cherished by innkeepers. If the inn has a special theme or the innkeeper is a collector of a specific item, send a surprise gift that can be displayed in the inn to remind the innkeepers of how their efforts are appreciated.

Q: What if an innkeeper presents me with a gift? Do I need to reciprocate in a like manner?

A: The most gracious way to reciprocate is with a heart-felt "thank you." Some people are natural "givers" and enjoy sharing with others. They are not seeking anything in return.

When a gift is given out of generosity, gratitude, or for no reason at all, accept it in the manner in which it is intended--and recycle the kindness to someone else when an opportunity arises. It always does.

B&B's Are Endless in their Uniqueness

Ashley River Bed & Berth
Charleston, SC

Inns
of Advisory Board Members

Bufflehead Cove Inn
Kennebunkport, ME

Iron Mountain Inn
Butler, TN

Beach Dreams B&B
Tybee Island, GA

Nicholson House
Athens, GA

Folly Castle Inn
Petersburg, VA

4 Rooster Inn
Tabor City, NC

Casa Sedona
Sedona, AZ

St. Francis Inn
St. Augustine, FL

John Penrose Virden House
Lewes, DE

Adams-Edgeworth Inn
Monteagle, TN

Mr. Mole B&B
Baltimore, MD

The Red Horse Inn
Landrum, SC

Prestwould B&B
Flat Top, WV

The Hope and Glory Inn
Irvington, VA

William Kehoe House
Savannah, GA

The Chalet Club
Lake Lure, NC

Web sites of Inns shown in "Innformation for Inngoers" section

Burke Manor Inn
(p. 134)
www.burkemanor.com

Victoria House B&B
(p. 135)
www.victoriahousebb.com

Melange B&B Inn and Gardens
(p. 136)
www.melangebb.com

Bonnie Castle
(p. 139)
www.communitynow.com/bonniecastle

The Duke Mansion
(p. 140)
www.dukemansion.org

Harmony House
(p. 142)
www.harmonyhousebb.com

Angel Arbor Bed and Breakfast Inn
(p. 144)
www.angelarbor.com

Hawkesdene House
(p. 145)
www.hawkbb.com

Inn on Covered Bridge Green
(p. 147)
www.coveredbridgegreen.com

Inn at Wintersun
(p. 149)
www.innatwintersun.com

Schell Haus
(p. 151)
www.schellhaus.com

Inn at Celebrity Dairy
(p. 152)
www.celebritydairy.com

Inn at Warner Hall
(p. 155)
www.warnerhall.com

Ashley River Bed & Berth
(p. 157)
bnbweb.com/ashleyriverbb/index.html

Basic Table Manners

*T*he understanding and application of good table manners makes a statement about one's background and experience. Some regions and individuals are more manners-conscious than others, and cultural differences must also be considered--especially when traveling abroad.

Whether having a country-style breakfast at a casual B & B, a lavish morning repast at an historic inn, or a sumptuous dinner at an upscale restaurant, good manners are important. Knowing which utensil to use when, as well as other basics, enables one to avoid being uneasy or self-conscious during mealtime. However, the most important "table rule" is mealtime pleasantness and consideration of those with whom the meal is being shared.

A brief overview of dining etiquette is bulleted below. Excellent Web sites are available providing detailed information on dining and social etiquette. Suggested links are listed on page 161. A reliable etiquette book (such as *Emily Post's Advice for Every Dining Occasion* by Elizabeth L. Post) is a must for every home library.

- After being seated at the table, place the napkin in your lap. After the meal is over, leave your napkin placed loosely next to your plate. It should neither be crumpled nor left on the chair.

- A correctly set table has utensils arranged in the order they are to be used--from the outside to the inside. For example, the outer fork is the first fork used (usually for a salad or an appetizer). This same rule applies to the spoons and knives (located on the right side of the plate). Glasses are placed to the right of the plate since the majority of folks are right-handed.

- Food is served from the left side, and plates are removed from the right side. Likewise, when passing food at the table, it is served to the right (received from one's left).

- When someone requests that the salt be passed, it is passed along with the pepper. While en route to the person making the request, it is not to be used by others.

- Straw-sipping is fine at fast-food restaurants, but straws are only to be used for stirring at nicer establishments.

- Unless you are adept at using chopsticks, only use one utensil at the time (except when cutting simultaneously, with a fork and knife). The empty hand is placed in the lap, *not* on the table.

- Once a utensil has been used, it must never touch the table again.

- A spoon is the utensil-of-choice for most fruit-type dishes (often the first breakfast course at inns).

- After eating food served in a compote or bowl, placed upon a plate, the spoon is placed on the plate (not left in the fruit or dessert dish).

Table Taboos

- Talking while food is in the mouth
- Talking on cell phones
- Blowing on hot foods or beverages
- Sopping bread into gravy or sauces
- Smoking
- Nose-blowing

- Picking teeth or using a toothpick
- Slurping soup
- Plate or bowl clanging (trying to scoop up last bites or drops)
- Putting elbows on the table or feet in the chair

Et Cetera

• Beepers and cell phones should be silenced during meal time at a restaurant or an inn. Many restaurants now request this courtesy.

• Even though requesting a take-home bag has become common place and acceptable at most restaurants (except for the most exclusive), this is not an appropriate request at an inn.

• In consideration of other paying guests, crying or misbehaving children need to be removed from a public dining area.

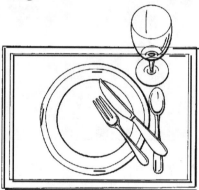

When finished eating, place your knife and fork in the position shown above. This signals that your plate is ready to be removed from the table.

Related Web Links

www.westernsilver.com/etiquette.html
www.cuisinenet.com/glossary/tableman.html
www.unlv.edu/Tourism/etiquette.html
www.visatablelinen.com
www.ryangrpinc.com/table_demo.html

If you have an etiquette-related question, you may send it to:
etiquette@emilypost.com

These Lowcountry oaks were once just two little "nuts,"
but they "held their ground" and survived the fury of Hurricane Hugo

Meet the Authors

Mother and Daughter--
Partners and Friends

Malyssa and Maxine Pinson
Mother's Day 2001

It is not who or what we were yesterday that matters.
It is who and what we are today,
and the hope of who and what we may become tomorrow.

Our Story

by Maxine Pinson

ৡ৵ৡ৵ৡ৵ৡ৵ৡ৵ৡ৵ৡ৵ৡ৵ৡ৵ৡ৵ৡ৵ৡ৵ৡ৵ৡ৵ৡ৵ৡ৵ৡ৵ৡ৵ৡ

*T*en years ago it would have been disastrous for my twelve-year-old daughter, Melissa, and me to have been left alone in a dangerous place like a kitchen. No doubt about it, one of us would have whopped the other one over the head with a frying pan within a matter of moments. The only uncertainty was who would get the first blow and who would win that day's battle.

If Melissa and I had to travel together, I sat behind the wheel up-front, and she sat in the mini-van's way-back yonder spot. The tension between the two of us was so caustic that we would not even sleep in the same room if we had to travel together. I would pay extra just to have a wall between us. Whenever I was home with Melissa alone at night, I slept with my bedroom door locked and a motion detector on. She did not have to worry about me going up to her room. It was such a disaster, I would not allow the exterminator to go into the sty for two years. Melissa and Myra, her guinea pig, lived like two little rats in a room that was knee-high with impossible-to-decipher stuff.

Five years ago, when Melissa was sixteen-years-old, I no longer had to worry about what would happen if we were left alone or daily battles. Melissa had become a teenage runaway. We had no clue where she was. There were times when we did not know if our daughter was dead or alive. Both possibilities were real, and each was haunting. Meanwhile, my husband, Bill, and I were facing another crisis. Our twenty-one year old daughter, Celia, was dying of a rare form of non-Hodgkin's lymphoma--mycosis fungoides. There were many days, during this time, when I was convinced I had died and gone to Hell. When I realized I was still roaming planet Earth, I decided Hell would probably be like a five-diamond resort in comparison. There were times when I wanted to die, prayed to die, asked others to pray for me to die. It was just that bad. I had neither the desire nor the energy for living a life that had become so painful.

More than anything in my life-to-date, Malyssa represents, to me, the manifestation of hope fulfillment and answered prayer. I am grateful that the many prayers (by me and so many others) for Malyssa's safe return and restoration were answered; I am thankful the prayers (prayed to a merciful God of love and grace) for my demise were unanswered.

Today I cannot imagine life without Malyssa, and I look forward to our time together. Seldom does a day pass that we do not see each other, chat by phone, or correspond by e-mail. Without Malyssa's support, encouragement, sensitivity, intelligence, sense-of-humor, keen eye-for-detail, affirmations, and confidence in my ability, *Lowcountry Delights* simply would not be. I love you, 'lyssa!

In 1999, shortly before her twentieth birthday, Melissa decided to change the spelling of her name to *Malyssa*. I sensed her desire to adopt a new spelling of her name was a statement of the "new" person she had become. I understood the message I felt my daughter was trying to convey, and I respected her decision to do so. The road Malyssa traveled was a difficult one, but I feel it has made her a stronger and more compassionate human being. She has become a woman I am proud to call "daughter" and "friend."

Malyssa and I worked, diligently, on *Lowcountry Delights* for nine months. During these busy months, Malyssa and I spent much time together (usually with Barrister and/or Chymarra napping nearby) collecting recipes, testing recipes, typing recipes, editing recipes, *screaming* at recipes. After being involved in publishing for almost twenty-five years, I understood the basics. However, compiling a cookbook/travel guide, as inclusive as *Lowcountry Delights*, entailed far more than I anticipated. By the time we went to press, I felt like a baby had been delivered. And, yes, all of our "labor pains" were negated by the overwhelming excitement of what we had jointly accomplished and the enthusiasm from others.

As we spent time working together on *Lowcountry Delights,* there were times when each of us inevitably did things annoying to the other. Yet, not once was a cross word or look exchanged, not even when we were working under a tight deadline and totally exhausted. Our relationship was tested in swirling waters and survived. Not only did our relationship survive, it flourished and became strengthened through our valuing of each other's gifts and goals.

In spite of the long hours and frustrations involved, neither of us would trade our experience of creating *Lowcountry Delights* for anything. Not all of our work was difficult, by any means. Our visits to delightful Lowcountry inns and restaurants provided the extra fuel we needed to keep on keeping on; the memories created, while on these trips, provided refueling when we needed rejuvenating.

Traveling together, one of us would drive while the other did cookbook work on one of our laptops. Unlike ten years ago, we both sat up front. We even enjoyed listening to the same music--well, most of the time. No more staying in separate rooms; in fact, we sometimes shared the same bed. During and after dinner each evening, we relaxed and enjoyed each other's company. Whether sitting in a back corner of an earthy-type eatery or on the upper veranda of an antebellum plantation home, we spent time sharing, laughing and talking about things of importance in our lives. During these times, I feel we learned a lot from each other, and we became closer than I ever thought possible.

So, what's the next chapter in our story? The completion of *52 Scrolls*. Malyssa's name will appear first on this book, because she is the one who conceived and initiated it. Her part is already complete; she is now sitting in the editor's chair reminding me of my deadline. The story behind *52 Scrolls* is one difficult to hear while remaining dry-eyed. I respect and appreciate Malyssa's courage and willingness to share her part of our story with others. Each of us hopes our experience will provide encouragement and hope for other daughters and mothers going through difficult times.

As far as we know, there is no book comparable to *52 Scrolls* in style or content. It is slated for release in 2004. Until then, Malyssa and I will continue making up for the years we lost by savoring every moment of the time we have together now.

"The present is a *gift*, and that is why it is called a *present*." This saying may appear trite, but it is full of truth.

Chymarra   Barrister

52 Scrolls

Malyssa Pinson
Maxine Pinson

The heart-wrenching and tumultuous journey
which follows the spontaneous combustion of a mother undergoing a "mid-life crisis"
as her younger daughter struggles with the crises of a troubled adolescence—
and the poignant experiences re-uniting them
into a close, loving, and accepting relationship cherished by each.

A must-read for any parent needing hope and encouragement
during years of teen-age turbulence

Slated for 2004
scrolls52@aol.com

Forthcoming Books

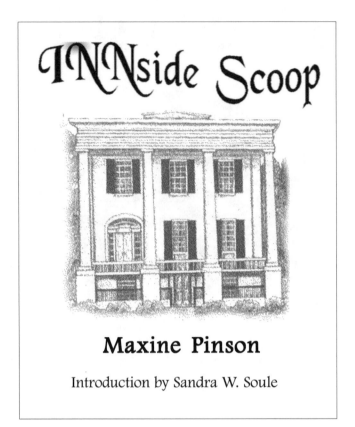

Maxine Pinson

Introduction by Sandra W. Soule

INNformation for INNgoers with "Inn Tales from Inn Trails"
(see example of an "inn tale" on p. 140)
INNside Scoop for INNkeepers
written for
The B&B and Country Inn MarketPlace Resource Guide

Published by
The B&B and Country Inn MarketPlace
Hickory, NC
1-800-871-8977
innsales@charter.net
www.innmarketing.com

Note: Scheduled to be released by December 2002
For more information, or to place an order,
visit www.the-innside-scoop.com/IS.htm

New England Delights Cookbook and Travel Guide

A New England version of Lowcountry Delights Cookbook and Travel Guide

(Slated for release in 2006)

Tripping Through Sunflower Fields
by
Maxine Pinson

An autobiographical account of emotional and spiritual survival through a decade of hell

(Slated for release in 2008)

Lessons I've Learned About Life
from My Computers and My Dogs
by
Maxine Pinson

A collection of inspirational reflections

(Slated...)

Note: *Lowcountry Delights, INNside Scoop,* and *New England Delights* will be periodically updated and revised with new "delights" and *inn*formation.

Web Sites

🙐🙐🙐🙐🙐🙐🙐🙐🙐🙐🙐🙐🙐🙐🙐🙐🙐🙐🙐🙐🙐🙐🙐🙐🙐🙐🙐🙐🙐

Free Bed and Breakfast Online Newsletters

(Subscribe online at Web Sites shown below)

The INNside Scoop

A bi-annual B & B newsletter
"Dedicated to the Discovery of Bed and Breakfast Getaways"
www.innsidescoop.com

BedandBreakfast.com Report

A bi-monthly B & B newsletter, edited by Sandy Soule
www.BedandBreakfast.com

Innformation for Innkeepers

Commentaries written by Maxine Pinson for *The B&B and Country Inn MarketPlace Resource Guide*
www.the-innside-scoop.com/marketguide.html

Bed and Breakfast Directories

www.innsidescoop.com   www.TravelGuides.com

www.BedandBreakfast.com   www.innmarketing.com/bbguide.htm

Where to Eat on the Inn Trail

www.thefoodscoop.com   www.eatinginsavannah.com

In Loving Memory of Celia Pinson Iskandar
(1974-1998)

www.the-innside-scoop.com/celia.htm

www.the-innside-scoop.com/howmuch.htm   www.rememberingcelia.com
www.the-innside-scoop.com/WHENBABY.html   www.rememberingcelia.com/video.html

Unhealthy Religiosity versus Healthy Spirituality

www.the-innside-scoop.com/unhealthy.html

www.the-innside-scoop.com/spirabuse.htm   www.the-innside-scoop.com/realjesus.htm

Parenting Editorials and Inspirational Writings by Maxine Pinson

www.the-innside-scoop.com/mpeditorials.htm

www.the-innside-scoop.com/abloom.htm   www.the-innside-scoop.com/waldo.htm
www.the-innside-scoop.com/aintme.htm   www.the-innside-scoop.com/mothersprayer.htm

Map, Index, Order Forms

The Lowcountry

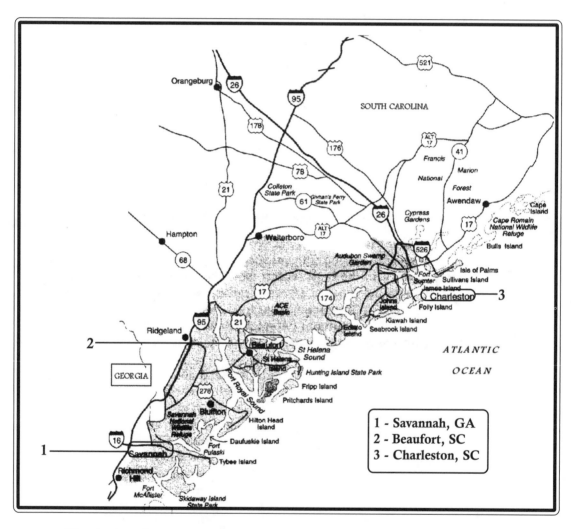

The the-lay-of-the-land in The Lowcountry (sometimes spelled Low Country)
is defined by its name. It is flat land, barely above sea level. It is also a region
impassioned with a sense-of-place which embodies a spirit as high as the land is low.

Index

Inns to Visit

〜〜〜〜〜〜〜〜〜〜〜〜〜〜〜〜〜〜〜〜〜〜〜〜〜

Restaurants to Try

〜〜〜〜〜〜〜〜〜〜〜〜〜〜〜〜〜〜〜〜〜〜〜〜〜

Order Form for *Lowcountry Delights*

Please ask in your local bookstore for Lowcountry Delights Cookbook and Travel Guide.
Or you may order it online from **www.amazon.com**
or **www.thefoodscoop.com/LowcountryDelights.html**.

Please send me _____ copies of

LOWCOUNTRY DELIGHTS @ $19.95 each   _____

(Georgia residents add $1.20 tax per book)   _____

Shipping and handling: Add $4.95 per book   _____

TOTAL   _____

VALUE PACK

Purchase 4 books for $72   _____

(Georgia residents add $4.32 sales tax)   _____

Shipping and handling: Add $10
(all 4 books shipped to same address)   _____

TOTAL   _____

Please make checks payable to: SSD, Inc.
(Payable in U.S. dollars only. No C.O.D.'s or Cash)

Name _____   Street _____

City _____ State _____ Zip _____ E-mail _____

May charge to major credit cards through Pay Pal account
(www.paypal.com)

Send order form to:
SSD, Inc. (LCD)
22 W. Bryan St.--PMB 202
Savannah, GA 31401

LCDcookbook@aol.com
www.thefoodscoop.com/LowcountryDelights.html

LOWCOUNTRY DELIGHTS

Cookbook/Travel Guide
featuring
Recipes from Favorite Lowcountry Inns & Restaurants

Special Section on
"INNformation for INNgoers"

by
Maxine Pinson & Malyssa Pinson
Editors of *The INNside Scoop*

Introduction by
Pamela Lanier

*Get your copy today
and order extra copies for gifts!*

Order Form for *Lowcountry Delights*

Please ask in your local bookstore for Lowcountry Delights Cookbook and Travel Guide.
Or you may order it online from **www.amazon.com**
or **www.thefoodscoop.com/LowcountryDelights.html**.

Please send me _____ copies of

LOWCOUNTRY DELIGHTS @ $19.95 each   _____

(Georgia residents add $1.20 tax per book)   _____

Shipping and handling: Add $4.95 per book   _____

TOTAL   _____

VALUE PACK

Purchase 4 books for $72   _____

(Georgia residents add $4.32 sales tax)   _____

Shipping and handling: Add $10
(all 4 books shipped to same address)   _____

TOTAL   _____

Please make checks payable to: SSD, Inc.
(Payable in U.S. dollars only. No C.O.D.'s or Cash)

Name _____ Street _____

City _____ State_____ Zip _____ E-mail _____

May charge to major credit cards through Pay Pal account
(www.paypal.com)

Send order form to:
SSD, Inc. (LCD)
22 W. Bryan St.--PMB 202
Savannah, GA 31401

LCDcookbook@aol.com
www.thefoodscoop.com/LowcountryDelights.html

LOWCOUNTRY DELIGHTS

Cookbook/Travel Guide
featuring
Recipes from Favorite Lowcountry Inns & Restaurants

Special Section on
"INNformation for INNgoers"

by
Maxine Pinson & Malyssa Pinson
Editors of *The INNside Scoop*

Introduction by
Pamela Lanier

*Get your copy today
and order extra copies for gifts!*

Order Form for *Lowcountry Delights*

Please ask in your local bookstore for Lowcountry Delights Cookbook and Travel Guide.
Or you may order it online from **www.amazon.com**
or **www.thefoodscoop.com/LowcountryDelights.html**.

Please send me _____ copies of

LOWCOUNTRY DELIGHTS @ $19.95 each   _____

(Georgia residents add $1.20 tax per book)   _____

Shipping and handling: Add $4.95 per book   _____

TOTAL   _____

VALUE PACK

Purchase 4 books for $72   _____

(Georgia residents add $4.32 sales tax)   _____

Shipping and handling: Add $10   _____
(all 4 books shipped to same address)

TOTAL   _____

Please make checks payable to: SSD, Inc.
(Payable in U.S. dollars only. No C.O.D.'s or Cash)

Name _____ Street _____

City _____ State _____ Zip _____ E-mail _____

May charge to major credit cards through Pay Pal account
(www.paypal.com)

Send order form to:
SSD, Inc. (LCD)
22 W. Bryan St.--PMB 202
Savannah, GA 31401

LCDcookbook@aol.com
www.thefoodscoop.com/LowcountryDelights.html

LOWCOUNTRY DELIGHTS

Cookbook/Travel Guide
featuring
Recipes from Favorite Lowcountry Inns & Restaurants

Special Section on
"INNformation for INNgoers"

by
Maxine Pinson & Malyssa Pinson
Editors of *The INNside Scoop*

Introduction by
Pamela Lanier

*Get your copy today
and order extra copies for gifts!*

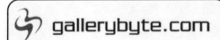

The B&B and Country Inn Marketplace

1-800-871-8977

innmarketing.com

Restaurants Recommended by The INNside Scoop
on
"The Inn Trail"

The Online River House Bakery

Savannah, GA

www.riverhouseseaood.com

RIVER HOUSE BAKERY ORDER FORM

THIS FORM MAY BE FAXED TO: 912-234-7007

Access Riverhouse Bakery
Online at
www.Riverhouseseafood.com

Price of Each Item Includes
Tax, Postage & Handling

Sour Cream Pound Cake $25.00

Fudge Walnut Pie $33.00

Georgia Pecan Pie $33.00 &

Praline Cheese Cake $60.00
(cheese cake overnight only)

PURCHASER'S NAME

DAY TIME PHONE NUMBER ( )

STREET ADDRESS   APT. #

CITY   STATE   ZIP

	ORDER TOTAL
Subtotal A	
Subtotal B	
Subtotal C	
Other orders	

PAYMENT ENCLOSED ☐ VISA ☐ MasterCard ☐ Novus

ENCLOSED IS MY CHECK OR MONEY ORDER MADE PAYABLE TO
THE RIVER HOUSE RESTAURANT IN THE AMOUNT OF $

ACCOUNT #

EXPIRATION DATE (month/year) / /

SIGNATURE

TOTAL AMOUNT

TODAY'S DATE / /   CLERK INITIAL   CREDIT AUTHORIZATION #

PLEASE SHIP TO THE FOLLOWING ADDRESS

NAME

DAY TIME PHONE NUMBER ( )

STREET ADDRESS   APT. #

CITY   STATE   ZIP

QTY.	ITEM DESCRIPTION	PRICE EACH	PRICE TOTAL

Message

FROM... (PRINT NAME)

ADD $30 FOR NEXT DAY AIR

SUBTOTAL "A"

Notes

Notes

Notes

Notes